THE
READER

"In this interesting collection, full of memorable details, John Michell commits many charming acts of political heresy against the received wisdoms of contemporary life, advocating by example where freedom still resides."

RICHARD HEATH, AUTHOR OF
SACRED NUMBER AND THE LORDS OF TIME

"Joscelyn Godwin has shown exceptional empathy with Michell's worldview in his judicious arrangement of the writings."

PATRICK HARPUR, AUTHOR OF *THE SECRET TRADITION OF THE SOUL* AND *THE PHILOSOPHERS' SECRET FIRE*

"Refreshingly original, yet genuinely grounded in tradition. John Michell is wise, mischievous, and amusing. He has expanded the frontiers of British sanity and enriches the lives of those who know him and his works."

RUPERT SHELDRAKE, AUTHOR OF
MORPHIC RESONANCE

"Forget trepanning, John Michell opened my third eye years ago. His revelations and the mysteries he touches upon are in my head forever—life would be dead dull and probably impossible without this extra and true dimension."

CANDIDA LYCETT GREEN, COAUTHOR OF
THE GARDEN AT HIGHGROVE

The Geometer No. 2.
Tempera painting of John Michell by Maxwell Armfield, ca. 1972.

THE  READER

WRITINGS and RANTS of
a Radical Traditionalist

SELECTED AND INTRODUCED BY
JOSCELYN GODWIN

Inner Traditions
Rochester, Vermont • Toronto, Canada

Inner Traditions
One Park Street
Rochester, Vermont 05767
www.InnerTraditions.com

Library of Congress Cataloging-in-Publication Data
Michell, John, 1933–2009.
  [Confessions of a radical traditionalist]
  The John Michell reader : writings and rants of a radical traditionalist / John Michell ; selected and Introduced by Joscelyn Godwin
      pages cm
  "Originally published in 2005 by Dominion Press under the title Confessions of a radical traditionalist: essays by John Michell" — Title page verso.
  Summary: "Deepest thoughts and musings of a 1960s countercultural icon"-- Provided by publisher.
  ISBN 978-1-62055-415-9 (pbk.) — ISBN 978-1-62055-416-6 (e-book)
  I. Godwin, Joscelyn, editor. II. Title.
  AC8.M475 2015
  082—dc23

                                                        2014038320

Printed and bound in the United States by Lake Book Manufacturing, Inc.
The text stock is SFI certified. The Sustainable Forestry Initiative® program promotes sustainable forest management.

10 9 8 7 6 5 4 3 2 1

Text design by Priscilla Baker and layout by Debbie Glogover
This book was typeset in Garamond Premier Pro with Frutiger LT Std and Nuptial Script LT Std as display fonts

Contents

PART IV
People

PART V
Sacred Cows

PART VI

Science

PART VII

Modern Madness

PART VIII

Apocalypsis

PART IX

Paradise of the Philosophers

INTRODUCTION
A Prophetic Vision

By Joscelyn Godwin

*I*n the dying years of the second millennium one of the few things that gave pleasure to this expatriate Englishman, when he let his mind's eye wander to what was left of his native land, was the thought that in an upper room somewhere in Notting Hill sat John Michell, writing another book, painting geometric figures, sharing a midnight feast with his visitors, or turning out another feuilleton for *The Oldie*.

It is not too much to say that John Michell was a prophet. Prophets do not foretell the future so much as warn what may come to pass if events continue on their present course. Nowadays this is so blindingly obvious that we hardly need prophets to tell it to us. But there is a rarer prophetic gift, which is the seeing of forms in what Plato called the "World of Ideas"—not the imaginary ideas of men and women, but the divine or daemonic ideas after which the material world is formed. Ezekiel saw the Chariot of the Most High; John the Divine saw the New Jerusalem; Mohammed in his night-journey passed through the planetary spheres and met the other prophets of his lineage. Such visions may be warnings too, but they also inspire confidence in the meaning and goodness of the cosmos; they enable us to imagine Paradise here and now and to adjust our lives in harmony with it.

Since his publication of the New Jerusalem canon in 1971, a prophetic vision of the latter kind was the foundation of all of John

Michell's writings, and his efforts were bent on bringing about its new descent as a source of joy, sanity, and sacred order in the world. These little essays were like the foam thrown off by the great wave of creative energy set in motion by this discovery, which Michell characterised, in all humility, as a revelation.

John Michell's other role was that of a guardian of tradition and its defender against the "new men" who mistrust everything ancient, beautiful, or suspect of elitism. These tinpot emperors come in for a sound chastisement in these pages, and it is not sheer malice to enjoy hearing someone shout that they are stark naked. The tradition that Michell defended has always been elitist, but not in the sense of favoring birth, money, or even brains. Instead, it fostered the quality, in every sphere, of being truly and comfortably what one is. In this sense, those who live by cultivating the land or by the careful work of their hands are more deserving of respect than media stars (even royal ones) or socialites. Moreover, Michell had a particular empathy for those at the bottom of the ladder who might have found their place in a more traditional social order but whom present-day conditions have made outsiders. He liked those who maintained their dignity and refused to compromise their own nature: tramps, canal folk, and "New Age travellers," or the West Africans and Asians of his London district.

In such an age gentle mockery is a better weapon than fulminating rants against the wrongness of things. Michell was gentle, though he knew where to stick the pin for maximum effect. He was a humorist— the kind who did not try to be funny, but simply was so because he saw things from angles that were unexpected and sometimes forbidden. Americans obviously value British humor for this last quality, living as they do under a rule of euphemism that would never, for example, call a magazine for senior citizens *The Oldie*.

Among the "forbidden" categories are those censored not out of moralism or sensitivity but because they are beyond the understanding, hence beneath the notice, of the experts. One example is calling into question William Shakespeare's authorship of the plays ascribed to him, to which Michell dedicated his longest book, *Who Wrote Shakespeare?* Alas, a plan for an exhibition on the subject in Stratford-upon-Avon proved unequal to the vested interests of the tourist industry. Long before that, Michell was a thorn in the side of the prehistoric archaeologists because he asked the wrong sort of questions and produced the wrong sort of evidence, while getting people much more excited about prehistoric remains than the experts ever could. If he was right, and there was a worldwide culture of high mathematical and technical achievement in the Stone Age, history books will have to be rewritten. But to give these experts their due, the trend of revision in prehistory has turned in Michell's favor, and the seeds planted in the popular mind by his early books flowered as the enthusiasts of the 1960s became the professors of the 1990s.

Moving from the past to the present, Michell was also an authority on things beyond the pale of respectability, "New Age travellers" of the intellectual world like flying saucers, crop circles, and weird phenomena that defy rational explanation. In his case, being an authority did not imply having the clue or the key to these, nor even believing that an explanation of them was possible. Such an admission is truly aggravating to the expert mind but no surprise to those who share Michell's esteem for America's great philosopher Charles Fort, who was content to say *Lo!* and unleash a flood of "damned" and inconvenient facts. The book *Phenomena,* written together with Robert Rickard and celebrating a long collaboration on the *Fortean Times,* collects instances of Teleportation, Stigmata, Fairies, Spontaneous Human Combustion, Falls of Liquids, and Mysterious Oozings, and so on, but without theories or explanations. This is of course the stuff of tabloids and urban legends, but when a serious and educated mind grapples with the evidence, the metaphysical consequences are quite momentous.

For all that he was a Platonist and a traditionalist, deeply enamored of a past that mirrored the divine order, Michell was also a radical of a typically English stamp. He belonged with William Blake, William Cobbett, William Morris, Henry W. Massingham, and those other defenders of Albion against its betrayers. Albion stands for the soul of Britain, which, like every race and nation, has its own potential perfection that enables it to sing its own melody in the chorus of humanity. It is no solution to the present cacophony to try to make them all mouth the same tune, whether composed in Washington or Brussels. But since the Reformation—so goes the story—the giant Albion has been in bondage and decay. His sickness is too old and too deep to be curable by mere conservatism or political action; only a radical, even a surgical cure will serve, one that people can support from the depth of their souls, not their pocketbooks.

One of John Michell's radical enterprises, the "Anti-Metrication Board," had a lasting effect on both sides of the Atlantic. He and his friends aroused popular sentiment through mockery of the bureaucrats and Eurocrats of the Metrication Board, and through events made for the media like the "Foot-Ball." One suspects that there was also some plain speaking in high places, with the result that Britain still measures in feet and miles, and weighed in pounds until 2002, when the new men made this a punishable offense; while in the United States, no one even tries to push metrication any further. But why should this matter? Why save the foot and refuse to "give an inch"? Michell's answer was that the English foot is the sole survivor of that universal system of ancient measures derived from the dimensions of the earth itself. As a prophet might warn, to wilfully give this up, after having surrendered so much else that roots us in the earth and in the past, can only herald further deracination and angst. And of course it is the old rival across the English Channel who first tried to foist on us the "atheistic, inaccurately measured metre."

Michell's many books and innumerable articles may seem to go off in all directions, but their unifying threads are evident enough if one can think like an artist, not an academic hemmed in by disciplinary boundaries. Consider the following chain of connections. A traditionalist's love of ancient remains led Michell to the toe of Cornwall to visit its stone circles and holy wells. In the process he ran across the work of the nineteenth-century Cornish artist John Blight, who recorded these old monuments in a book which he dedicated to the then Prince of Wales and Duke of Cornwall (later Edward VII). Likewise, Michell opened his book *The Old Stones of Land's End* with a dedicatory poem to Prince Charles, who was just then emerging as a defender of traditional values. Michell then wrote a life of Blight, *A Short Life at the Land's End,* which tells the story of the artist's early promise, his exploitation by wilier men, and his descent into madness. (Michell would later develop the genre in *Eccentric Lives and Peculiar Notions.*) Stone circles of course suggest Stonehenge, a key item in the quest for the lost canon that began in *The View over Atlantis* (revised as *The New View over Atlantis*) and continued through *City of Revelation* (revised as *The Dimensions of Paradise*), and *Ancient Metrology.* The suppression of the traditional summer solstice celebration at Stonehenge called forth one of Michell's "Radical Traditionalist Papers," *Stonehenge, Its History, Meaning, Festival, Unlawful Management, Police Riot '85 & Future Prospects,* a stirring anti-establishment tract; while *Megalithomania* chronicled the lovers and haters of megaliths in the past, and *A Little History of Astro-Archaeology* theories of their cosmic connections.

Not far from Stonehenge is Glastonbury, another piece of the canonical jigsaw, which produced the prophetic *New Light on the Ancient Mysteries of Glastonbury.* An aura of openness to ancient British mysteries had hung around the place since the turn of the twentieth century, and Michell's *The View over Atlantis,* his "Art and Imagination" book *The Earth Spirit: Its Ways, Shrines and Mysteries,* and his guidebook *The Traveler's Key to Sacred England* had helped to revive it in recent times. Beginning in the 1980s, the same region of Southwest England was also the centre for the phenomenon of the crop circles, which soon developed into designs of extraordinary ingenuity and beauty. Michell helped to found a journal devoted to the phenomenon, *The Cerealogist,* which was so wittily written and wisely edited that I, and others, always read it from cover to cover the day it arrived. Meanwhile I recall that Michell's very first book, *The Flying Saucer Vision,* associated the UFOs with ancient sites and straight lines across the landscape, and that UFO phenomena accompanied some of the crop circles. The straight lines would reappear as the famous "ley lines" first publicised in *The View over Atlantis,* which thousands of happy hikers in the 1970s traced on Ordnance Survey maps: the same people, or at least the same types, who would later be found measuring crop circles and arguing in the pubs of Glastonbury. Michell went on from the study of leys to wider-ranging alignments across the British Isles and beyond, which he realised were part of an ancient scheme of surveying the land, dividing it, and placing its sacred centres. In a flash of inspiration he associated this with the twelve "perpetual choirs" that are said to have sung in Glastonbury and other abbeys, giving rise to the book written with Christian Rhone, *Twelve-Tribe Nations and the Science of Enchanting the Landscape,* and shortly after to *At the Center of the World: Polar Symbolism Discovered in Celtic, Norse and Other Ritualized Landscapes.*

When it is known that Michell also painted and wrote verses, the word "dilettante" comes to mind; but here, too, his creativity was part and parcel of the single vision that I am trying to capture. Far from being "self-expression" in modernist mode, Michell's recent paintings were highly disciplined geometrical illuminations based on Platonic mathematics and other archetypal forms; a prototype appeared on the cover of *The Dimensions of Paradise,* illustrating a version of the New Jerusalem diagram with its twelve colored gemstones. *Euphonics: A Poet's Dictionary of Sounds* is a book of verses and essays on the audible qualities of the letters of the alphabet, illustrated by the cartoonist Merrily Harpur. Disguised as highbrow frivolity, its basis is equally Platonic: the idea that the names of things embody something of their inmost quality. A line of association strikes off here to *Simulacra: Faces and Figures in Nature,* in which Michell presented photographs of animal, vegetable, and mineral things that look like something else. It seems almost childish, but back in the Renaissance, when the doctrine of signatures was understood, it stood to reason that like will be marked with like. These books are both Platonic and Fortean because they remind us that the world is full of wondrous coincidences that we miss if, in our rationality, we think it insignificant that some rocks have faces or that the letter B resembles a bum, boobs, and balls.

A similarly eccentric thread unites Michell's more polemical activities. To those who can see only two sides to every issue, some of his shifts are incomprehensible and have lost him friends. In 1977 he issued a Radical Traditionalist Paper in support of the defendant in the *Gay News* trial, the first and last trial for blasphemy in modern Britain. The magazine had published a poem spoken by Jesus's supposed lover and mentioning "that great cock." Michell gleefully demonstrated that *To Represent Our Savior as "that great cock" Is Not Blasphemy but Eternal and Christian Orthodoxy:* a treatment fully within the tradition of the "phallic school" of symbolism, from the eighteenth-century antiquarian Payne Knight to the Rosicrucian pretender Hargrave Jennings (though the homosexual community failed to appreciate the gesture). Yet when Salman Rushdie became the victim of the Iranian *fatwa* for blasphemy in his *Satanic Verses,* Michell wrote another Rad-Trad Paper, *Rushdie's Insult,* which must have been the only anti-Rushdie broadside fired by a non-Muslim. Michell later withdrew the paper, but I mention it because the intention behind it is more timely than ever: "The object of the pamphlet," Michell wrote in his withdrawal, "was to combat the flood of anti-Islamic passions and propaganda unleashed in Europe and America by Rushdie's apologists." The most vocal of these apologists were the leading lights of the British literary establishment, complacent modernists to a man and hence natural targets of Michell's scorn. A third potential scandal never broke: it was the "little red book" entitled *The Hip-Pocket Hitler,* in which Michell gathered, after the current fashion of books of aphorisms by Mao, Ghaddafi, and other dictators, all the quotes and quips of Adolf Hitler's table-talk that sound most witty, sensible, and pleasantly provocative. Without knowing the identity of their speaker, the kind of person who enjoys Michell's writing would agree with almost all of them. Then awkward questions arise: Are they less wise and witty because of who said them? Was Hitler, in some part of his character, one of us? What appears as the naughtiness of a grown-up schoolboy turns out to be a contribution to higher education, as all of Michell's work is, with the intention of making us more thoughtful, less confident in the experts, and less receptive to political agendas sugar-coated in moralism.

That received myths and unsubtle beliefs can do real harm to mind and soul is one reason for Michell's diatribe against Darwinism. American readers should keep in mind that Christian fundamentalism is of no significance whatever in Britain: all that was done away with long ago, and the United Kingdom, like most of Europe, is virtually post-Christian territory. Consequently Darwinism does not have the same iconic value as it does in America, as a bastion against biblical literalism and "creation science." Darwinism, as Michell saw it, is the pseudo-religion of the new men, sanctified by the Hawkings and Dawkinses: a religion that never questions the shaky theory that man is descended from lemurs through a mindless and godless process. To be a Darwinist—and Charles Darwin, to give him credit, was not one of them—cuts one off from any possibility of sharing in Michell's prophetic vision; but then so do bibliolatry and fundamentalism. As always, Michell's solutions lie off-centre, neither to the Left nor the Right, but in the third dimension: the Above.

Saddened by the spectacle of what the clinging to religious differences has done to two once sacred nations, Michell turned his attention to those perennially running sores, Ireland and Israel. With a boldness of vision that is shocking to those who prefer either to take sides or to put it all out of their minds, he proposed a new order for both lands, in the paper *The Concordance of High Monarchists of Ireland: The Pattern of the Future* and the book *The Temple at Jerusalem: A Revelation*. He showed that the ancient divisions of Ireland and of the city of Jerusalem were laid out according to the sacred canon of measures and harmony that once held every island and nation in a blessed enchantment. Michell surely believed that with God all things are possible and that the enchantment could descend again, but only under a spiritual authority imposed from above, personified in the traditional institution of sacred kingship. The less sanguine reader can take these proposals in the spirit of Plato's *Republic:* as ideas that cannot manifest on earth so long as the human material remains what it is, but which can serve as a guiding light to men of good will. Moreover, as the last gathering of these *Oldie* essays shows, there is always the possibility for the individual to create a present Paradise and to attune his own microcosm, at least, with the greater harmony.

In selecting these 108 essays from ten years of contributions to *The Oldie,* I have jumbled them chronologically but united them thematically. John Michell was not responsible for this arrangement, nor for the fact that Americans will have never heard of some of the events and people to whom they allude. This is, after all, journalism. But a public that can enjoy thirty-year-old British sitcoms with their incomprehensible allusions and Anglicisms should have no trouble appreciating it.

JOSCELYN GODWIN, musicologist and historian of ideas, teaches at Colgate University. He was born in Kelmscott, Oxfordshire, England, and has written widely on the Western esoteric tradition. He is the translator of the 1499 architectural-erotic novel *Hypnerotomachia Poliphili.* Godwin's books include *Harmonies of Heaven and Earth, Music and the Occult, Arktos: The Polar Myth, The Theosophical Enlightenment, The Pagan Dream of the Renaissance, The Real Rule of Four, Athanasius Kircher's Theatre of the World,* and *Atlantis and the Cycles of Time.* He lives in Hamilton, New York.

PART I

The Good Old Days

1

Why Are We So Short of Time?

December 1995

Time goes quicker as you get older. When you are a child, an empty hour with nothing interesting to do in it is torture and a wasted day is a tragedy, but when you are old you can nod through a day and hardly notice that it has gone. An old chap said to me that he felt he had only just got out of his weekly bath when it was time for the next one.

The reason for that, I suppose, is that in childhood each moment brings a new experience, so your day stretches out as a long chain of sensations, whereas by the time you are old everything is so familiar that life slips by like a dream. It is one of nature's mercies that we are given a long-drawn-out youth and a short, painless old age.

I suspect, however, that these days there is more to it than that. Everyone now complains about not having enough time, and the general impression is that time itself has speeded up, and there are not as many minutes in the hour as there used to be.

Reading about the life of Mr. Gladstone I was struck by how much more he was able to do than anyone could possibly manage today. As Prime Minister he not only ran the entire British Empire and controlled affairs throughout much of Europe, but he was a prodigious reader and a leading classical scholar, writing learned volumes on Homer and publishing translations from Latin, Greek, German, and Italian. The list of his works in the British Library catalogue runs to no less than thirty pages.

He made constant speeches, elegantly phrased and lasting for up to five hours, and at the same time he was active in charities and religious movements, writing long letters to friends, going for long walks, looking after his family, and attending social functions, while still having time in the evenings to redeem fallen women. All this was done without a telephone or typewriter, and of course there were no computers then, without which people nowadays cannot even run a little sweetshop.

Then there was Sir Walter Scott. I have just started reading his novels, beginning, since I am interested in the Shetland Islands, with *The Pirate,* and already my outlook on life has been completely changed. In the sixty-one years of his life he wrote more than sixty books, including a nine-volume *Life of Napoleon* containing as many words as five of his long, elaborate novels put together.

No one has the time to read, let alone write, all that today. And it was not in his eyes the most important part of his career. He wished to be seen as a Scottish laird and performed all the duties and functions of that rank, building himself a baronial mansion, administering local justice, aiding his dependents, and receiving all kinds of visitors.

Parties of unexpected sightseers distracted him throughout the day, and he was constantly travelling in search of ancient lore, as an official inspector of lighthouses or as companion to foreign dignitaries. He wrote mostly before breakfast, leaving the rest of the day for other business, including a publishing enterprise, which incurred such enormous debts that he had to spend the rest of his life working to stave off creditors.

What has happened to time? Why is there now so little of it compared to the amount there used to be?

I have not the space to go properly into those questions, but a brief answer is that it is because of all those delusive instruments that are supposed to save time—computers, Internets, and so on. I shall never let one of those demonic things into my house, and I advise readers who have them to throw them out, together with the television set. That way you will have time for family life and leisure enough to read the entrancing novels of Sir Walter Scott.

2
Fireside Wisdom

January 1992

*P*ondering, as I often do, the question of how and when the world went mad, I recently made an important breakthrough. It was to do with the displacement of the hearth or fireplace.

The oldest and most satisfactory form of dwelling is the "primitive hut." Made simply of sticks, stones, mud, or whatever is to hand, it has a circular wall and a conical thatched roof with an opening at the top to let out smoke from the central fire. Its inhabitants sit round a square hearthstone where the fire warms a cooking pot suspended from a chain.

Anthropologists have found that this practical arrangement is everywhere seen as a cosmological scheme. Within the circumference of the wall, representing a limited universe, the hearthstone is the body of the earth, with four corners and four directions, and it is the seat of Hestia the (h)earth goddess, whose energies are concentrated in the central fire. The chain is the world-pole, the link between heaven and earth and the means of intercourse with gods and spirits. Conversation is directed into the fire while dreams and images are drawn out of it. It is too smoky to read or look at pictures. Eyes and minds are concentrated upon the focal point. In that situation, sitting in friendly company around a fire on which a pot is simmering, one is likely to feel "centred" and at ease.

We still speak of sitting "around" a fire, even though the modern fireplace is on one side of a rectangular room and we actually sit in front of it. With this new arrangement the influence of the old cosmological imagery became inactive and minds became less centred. Now even the wall-fire has been abolished from many homes, and the main focus is provided by the electric cooker or flickering television set.

Thus the traditional cosmology is no longer represented by its domestic symbols and a new, secular, restless, uncentred worldview has taken its place.

Focus, meaning a centre which receives and emits rays of light, is the Latin name for the central fireplace. The fire not only warms but, as a symbol, illuminates the corresponding images of a centre to each of our own beings and of a world-centre, which is divine, eternal, and unchanging.

For calming the mind and restoring it to its proper order there is no substitute for a centrally placed hearth. There is much comfort in our modern domestic machinery—gramophone, television, central heating—but with these accessories we are not exactly focussed. We are distracted, torn from the realities of dreams and imaginings centred upon our own hearths and minds, and aimlessly drifting in a sea of alien fantasies.

Modern house-builders have given us high levels of convenience and hygiene while ignoring the psychological necessity of a focus; and through the absence of a cosmologically significant centre our minds have become unbalanced. It is ironic that so many places are called art centres, culture centres, and so on, when they have no centre at all but slop around on erratic tides of fashion and faddery.

They should put a pole up the middle, light a fire at its base, make that a symbol of eternal beauty and truth, and concentrate the minds of their inmates upon it, thus uplifting the standard of their artworks.

Now I know how the world went mad. We knocked the centre out of it, and ever since we have been fumbling around looking for it, mistaking our own or other people's obsessions for the real thing.

3

The Deserted Village

February 1997

*T*he all-time popular favourite among English poems is *The Deserted Village,* first published in 1770. That is just my opinion and readers will have their own ideas, but I am on firmer ground in claiming that Oliver Goldsmith's poem has had more influence than any other. It tells of the idyllic country life that he remembered from his Irish childhood and later beheld in the villages of England. From the pious parson and the all-knowing schoolmaster to the wise elders in the pub and the young, independent cottagers, everyone was simple, happy, and honestly employed. They lived well on their native products, by their own skills and culture, with no surplus wealth for needless luxuries. Goldsmith insisted that he actually saw this idyll, this recently lost Golden Age, and that it was just as his poem described it. He was equally firm in identifying the cause of its sudden destruction—through the new wealth engendered by trade, industry, and capitalism.

The Deserted Village was William Cobbett's favourite poem. A generation after Goldsmith, he too remembered the perfection of old England under the peasant economy, and fought a life-long rearguard battle on behalf of its remnants. That memory seems to have a life of its own. People have always been telling their children how beautiful and peaceful the countryside was in their youth and how hideous it has become since, and the children have handed down the same story. In pursuit of that memory, idealists through the last two centuries have started back-to-the-land movements, setting up craft colonies, garden cities, or hippy communities in defiance of the economic forces that overwhelmed "sweet Auburn." Yet those forces are still in the ascendancy, even more firmly than before. Has it all been just a dream? Is the idea of a quite recent Golden Age no more than a nostalgic illusion that deepens as one gets older? Or was Goldsmith right in asserting that there was such an age, and now it has gone?

Obviously the rural economy has changed in our time. In the East Anglian village of my youth there were tradesmen and craftsmen. Now there is a post-office, stores, and precious little else. The local accent is no longer dominant in the pub, and the people you see there are more likely to be in advertising or film-making than flint-knappers* or tillers of the soil. The place has been completely taken over. New money from outside has destroyed the old values and driven out the younger villagers, just as Goldsmith saw happening in his time.

There is something odd about this. How can the village, described in Goldsmith's poem as utterly ruined, have survived up to the present, while providing to each generation an image of first a paradise and then a desolation? No doubt today's children will grow up with an ideal memory of my spoilt village, and will tell their children how lovely it used to be. It is now indeed better preserved, more trim and orderly than in the old days, and many of the new people are lively and interesting, practicing arts and crafts and following the guidance of *Country Living*. To those who have eyes to see, meaning children, it is a very plausible image of paradise. In that, I am sure, lies a very important secret. Poets and seers have often observed that paradise on earth is the essential reality, but we have lost the habit of living in it. By an effort of will we can train ourselves to regain that reality. It is a

---

*[craftsmen who shape flint into tools. —*Ed.*]

gradual process but rewarding from the very first moment one decides to try it. The village is not such a desert after all. Its economics have changed, radically, but its people are the same in spirit as the good-hearted, independent-minded English folk who enjoyed the pleasures of sweet Auburn.

4

Fear and Loathing
of the Greens

May 2001

*A*n article in the *Times* caught my eye. It was by Oliver Walston, who described himself as an East Anglian barely baron. In the bit that attracted me he was harking back to the olden days, "when the fields of Britain were filled with happy, smiling farmworkers who laughed, sang, and drank draft cider as they brought in yet another bumper harvest." I suppose he meant draught cider, drawn from the cask rather than from a draft on someone's bank. But, pedantry aside, I was pleased by his description. It reminded me of De Valera's beautiful historic speech at the foundation of the Irish Republic, where he looked forward to

A land whose countryside would be bright with cosy homesteads, whose fields and villages would be joyous with the sounds of industry, with the romping of sturdy children, the contests of athletic youths, the laughter of comely maidens; whose firesides would be the forums for the wisdom of serene old age. It would, in a word, be the home of a people living the life that God desires that men should live.

Glowing with these sentiments, I went on with Walston's article but, oh dear, he did not mean it like that at all. He was being sarcastic. And the target of his coarse wit was the Greens. These people, he said, react to every modern farming disaster with an "organic orgasm." They want to do away with chemicals and fertilisers, and demand healthy, natural-tasting food, produced locally. "The Greens," said Walston, "are religious fanatics who would like to 'turn back the clock to a golden age.'" His own conclusion was that traditional farming is obsolete in modern Europe. The remaining "peasants" should become salaried park-keepers, allowing "the large hard-nosed commercial producers" free range over the rest of the country.

The context of the article was this year's outbreak of foot-and-mouth disease and the doubts that it raised about the viability of modern commercial agriculture. To stifle these doubts many similar articles were commissioned. Another I saw was by *The Telegraph*'s Matt Ridley, the North Country landowner who is well known for his infallibly wrong-headed opinions. He denied that modern practices were in any way to blame for the disease and reaffirmed his support for centralised, chemical, high-tech agri-business. It is, he declared, the only option. There is no turning back.

The more I read of this stuff the more convinced I became that there is an option and a turning back, and the sooner we take them the better. There was a nasty, menacing tone in some of those articles, Walston's in particular, that jarred upon my liberal susceptibilities. His attack on the Greens was so intemperate and vulgar that I am surprised the *Times* published it. What is so wrong about wanting fresh food and a human-scale economy? Instead of selling beef to America and importing it back via Timbuktu, why should we not do things simply, producing our own kindly reared animals and delicious garden vegetables, while preserving the traditional amenities of rural life? These are practical options, which it seems harmless to consider. But to the barely barons, the chemical magnates, and all those involved in the commercial takeover of the world agriculture, these ideas are heretical, even wicked.

That is why our man was so vicious about the organic movement and the Greens. They threaten to bust his racket.

Walston and his fellows are playing a dangerous game and staking our whole future upon it. They are taking on Nature, and that is a war that no one can ever win, for it is also a war against human nature and against God. If they go on like this there will be an almighty crash, after which reality will gradually reassert itself. By reality I mean that ideal existence, which, even when it is not apparent, remains constant in our dreams and romances. There is no picture of it, but it is far more like De Valera's vision than Oliver Walston's.

What has happened
to time? Why is there now so little of it
compared to the amount there used to be?
I have not yet looked properly into those

5

Staying Put
and Rushing About

March 2001

My grandmother used to say, "You young people are so restless, always rushing about from here to there. When we were girls it was so lovely at home that we were never wanted to leave, even to get married. Aunt F— cried when her husband took her away."

It is true that we were always rushing about, in dangerous motor cars, with desperate episodes of drunken driving. I shudder now to think of it. In Granny's youth there were no motors, so staying put was the normal thing in the country. But later it became a sort of disgrace, and now everyone keeps going away, rushing about in planes and boasting about their constant, far-flung travels as if there were virtue in their restlessness.

Americans are at the forefront of this movement—they are said to move house on average every three or four years—but all our colonials are the same. Unable to settle properly in the lands they took from the natives, with no traditional ties to the landscapes they were born in, they are condemned to wander, and that is why we have the pleasure of so many overseas visitors each year.

A few generations ago, when the enchantment of old England still lingered in country districts, most villagers had never been farther than the local market town, and many had never set foot outside their own parish. It was like in that Chinese poem about the idyllic community, where nothing unusual ever happened, where it was so quiet that they could hear dogs barking in the next village, which none of them had ever gone to.

One of my hobbies is collecting examples of good people who have enjoyed long lives, happy and complete, while scarcely moving an inch from where they were born. It began during the Falklands war, when a reporter said that he had met islanders in the outlying "campo" who had never been to the capital, Port Stanley, in their whole lives. Then, in the way these things happen, I heard from another journalist something even more extraordinary, that on the island of St. Helena, which is only ten miles across at most, there were rustics who had never been to their only town, Jamestown.

Best of all was the example of staying put which I came across in a book about the Faroe Islands by two highly informed and entertaining sub-Arctic women, Liv K. Schei and Ounnie Moberg (they also wrote the best modern book on Shetland). On the remotest island of the Faroes, Fugloy, barely two miles long and with two small villages, they heard of a woman who lived in one of the villages and had never bothered to visit the other one. Nor had she ever left the island. On her seventieth birthday the treat she asked for was to be shown the next village. It was a few minutes' walk and she thoroughly enjoyed the novelty.

A traditional view of such lives is that they are compensations for hyperactivity in a previous existence. At the end of Plato's *Republic* is a description of souls destined for rebirth, where each was allowed to choose the pattern of its next life. The foolish among them grabbed lives of wealth and power only to find too late that they ended nastily. Among the last souls to pick a life was Ulysses, whose former career was of constant rushing around. Most of the lives had gone, but thrown away in a corner he found the life of a quiet, retiring country gentleman. That, he said, would have been his choice if he had had first pick. So in one life you rush around, and in the next you stay put.

That is only a story, but it is the best one you are likely to find that accounts for the co-existence in human nature of those opposite types that you see in children, the one that sits there happily and the one who simply cannot keep still.

6

Victoria's Enchanted Realm

February 2001

Q ueen Victoria died one hundred years ago this January, and I still miss her. Not that I knew her, of course, or even existed in her time, but her influence was so powerful that it long outlived her. In my childhood some sixty years ago the code of behaviour one was supposed to live by was properly called Victorian. One source of that code was the Bible and another was the romance of King Arthur. Putting them together, the Victorians conceived an ideal type of modern human being: the fair, kind, and honourable Christian gentleman. What a lovely image. No one could actually live up to it, but that is the nature of an ideal. It was so attractive that the Victorians made it their standard in art and life, and they longed for other nations to share it. Several generations from all classes in these islands travelled throughout the world, enlightening the natives, bringing them order, justice, railways, manly sports, and, above all, the gentlemanly ideals of Protestant Christianity. Some people were grateful for this benign intervention, but others denounced it as a demonstration of white man's arrogance. That is what happens when you try and do good. "Blessed are ye when men shall revile you."—Matthew 5:11.

As the twentieth century dies it is tempting to compare it with its Victorian predecessor, but no one likes to because it is too embarrassing.

26

Try, for example, comparing the Great Exhibition with the Millennium Dome, or Landseer with Damien Hirst. Or, more directly, consider the stability and comfort of Victorian life while experiencing the squalor that has replaced it. But it is no use moaning. The interesting question about Queen Victoria is how she did it. How did she so enchant her kingdom that, despite all mundane hardships, most of her subjects followed her moral leadership, were contented with their lot, and would give their lives in her service? She did not do it by herself, of course, but through certain counselors, including her husband, Albert, and her prime minister Disraeli, who were initiated in the ancient science of statecraft. This is an esoteric subject, unknown to the tyrants and upstarts who rule widely today, but practised by the wise and learned in every period of good governance. Its purpose is to cast a spell over a nation, creating an atmosphere of security and well-being. Victoria's advisers were in the same tradition as those who previously, in the time of Good Queen Bess, spin-doctored her reign to present an image of the Virgin goddess with her court of heroes. And before them, at different times and places in antiquity, were the philosopher-kings whose rule was simply by myth, music, and custom.

Today things are different. The world has become disenchanted, the old myths have lost their power, cultures and customs are fading, and there is no assurance of continuity in anything. Twenty years ago there were people called futurologists who predicted all sorts of wondrous things—that by now we would be living on the moon, served by robots, and so on, nothing of which has happened. That proves that we can no longer foresee the future, even the year ahead, so we are in the hands of the gods. This was acknowledged by our present Queen in her Christmas speech. Her position, she reminded us, is essentially religious; she is responsible to God for all forms of worship within the kingdom. I have criticised Elizabeth before for her inertia while English rights and customs are eroded, but this speech was her justification. In times such as these, when man-made chaos has grown beyond human resolution, the only practical step is to invoke divine guidance. Any individual who does so is more likely to find purpose and happiness in life, and the same is true of any nation. It was right and timely for the Queen to speak out in that way. The gods, as Plato observed, often choose the most unlikely people to utter the most important truths.

7

A Good Protestant?
How and Why

October 1997

*M*y father was a firm Protestant, did not care for the Pope, and regarded foreigners with suspicion. I grew up to sympathise with that attitude, and my prejudiced inclination was toward the simple, kindly Church of England in contrast to the pretentiousness of Catholicism. When I heard that we Protestants were the true heirs to our primordial Celtic Church, which perpetuated Druidic doctrines and the traditions that had been upheld on this island since the year dot, I believed that too. Then I read *The History of the Protestant Reformation* by that good English Protestant, William Cobbett (a tutelary hero of *The Oldie*), and my eyes were opened. Cobbett's catch phrase, repeated throughout his book, is that the Reformation "was engendered in beastly lust, brought forth in hypocrisy and perfidy, and cherished and fed by plunder, devastation, and by rivers of innocent English and Irish blood." He proved it in detail, and everything I have since read confirms it. Before the Reformation the Catholics maintained a very plausible version of Merrie England. The monks and abbots owned about a sixth of all the land in Britain, and under their management the rural economy flourished as it has never done since. In every village expert craftsmen practised their skills and passed them on to the new generation. A succession of fairs and feast days marked the seasons of the year, and though many country people were illiterate, their songs, stories, and wide, expressive vocabulary were from a culture more genuine and deep-rooted than can be acquired through book-learning.

This somewhat idyllic state was shattered by the Protestant henchmen of that prototype of Stalin, Henry VIII ("that old wife-killer" as Cobbett called him). Every ancient home of religion was destroyed, their lands were confiscated and privatised, and, instead of gentle Father Abbot, a parvenu aristocrat exploited the people whom his predecessors had nourished. A spell was broken, a culture liquidated, and the old, God-centred saying, "all for One and One for all," was replaced by "every man for himself."

The Protestants believed that people should live by reason rather than superstition. This is a fine-sounding ideal and many great thinkers have adopted it. Francis Bacon wanted to codify all knowledge, subordinate it to the Bible, and make it the syllabus for a new, God-fearing, rational-minded generation of Protestant Englishmen. There is just one flaw in this, but it is fatal. Religion and rationalism are not friendly to each other. When Protestantism gave birth to Socialism and compulsory education, God was pushed out of the classroom and in came Marx and Darwin and a host of atheistic fads that have confused everyone ever since.

Most people do not want to think for themselves, and it is cruel to insist on it. Popular demand is for a skilled and satisfying occupation, plenty to eat and drink, and a succession of entertainments and good parties. This is what the Catholics provided, and to these they added sound religious doctrines, which, if more or less observed, gave you a clear conscience and a passage to Heaven. It was of course an illusion or, properly speaking, an enchantment, because the key to it all was the chanting of the monks in their abbey churches. This was a trick they learnt from the Celts, whose perpetual, day-and-night chants in the choirs all over Britain maintained harmonious, lawful order within their realms. The Protestants smashed that enchantment, and it is impossible to put Humpty Dumpty together again. So if you were born into the Church of England you might as well stay there. One day, no doubt, the Grail will be restored and the heavenly Jerusalem revealed, but in these times of chaos the only honest policy is to admit that you are totally confused and ignorant. That is what is meant by being a good Protestant.

8

Kings of Glory

June 1995

A president may be a very respectable and worthy person, but countries under a president rather than a king and queen are constitutionally second rate. Even little girls know that, for they are natural princesses and are entitled to marry handsome princes rather than the uncouth sons of Chairman Somebody. Poetically and spiritually kings are real whereas presidents are merely human conventions.

In fairy stories there has never been a Chairman of Elfland. Nature herself is monarchical. The birds have the eagle as their king, the beasts have the lion, British butterflies defer to the Purple Emperor. No one refers to gold as the President of Metals, and not even republican Christians call Jesus the President of Glory.

Kingship is a religious office and its purpose is to uphold the sacred laws and standards of a nation. That is why it has been so widely rejected in this century. Ever since the triumph of Darwinism, atheistic science has denied the existence of divine standards, replacing them with man-made theories, which are merely fads and mostly false and evil. The scientific way of thought leads naturally to atheistic dictatorship; Hitler, Stalin, Mao, Pol Pot, and Enver Hoxha are the typical twentieth-century rulers. Modernism set them up in its own image, and everything they created was a faithful reflection of the demonic spirit that has dominated our era.

The complete contrast between sacred kingship and secular despotism is clearly displayed in their respective monuments. Since we were last in touch I have been to Albania, where the old houses have everywhere been replaced by socialistic apartment blocks, hideously ruined and ill adapted for the requirements of goatherds; while the central city, Elbasan, has been made into a stinking health hazard by gigantically poisonous Chinese steel works. This assault on his own people was carried out by a great, fat, smirking old Stalinist queer, the aforementioned E. Hoxha (pronounced "Hodger").

This murderous menace, who would not let anyone keep even one private hen, was supported by Churchill and, largely through the treachery of Philby, was able to exterminate the opposition, the supporters of good King Zog, whose benevolent rule was terminated by the Italian Fascists. Zog's successor, King Leka, and his lovely Australian queen, Susan, await recall to their legitimate realm, but the Albanian imagination has been so traumatised by Hodgerism that it no longer retains the high image of a monarch, and poor King Leka seems destined to die as he has lived, a king over the water.

At Tsarskoe Selo, outside St. Petersburg, is the monument that best exemplifies the ideals of kingship. The Tsar's palace there is a magnificent product of art and culture, the very antithesis of communistic vulgarity. It is magnificent on the human scale, befitting the simple-living, God-fearing family that inhabited it and the good old Father of All Russia who after breakfast would potter around the garden and feed the birds by the lake. Even the misery of his time was on the human scale and different in quality from the mass-produced misery created by his demonic successors.

Whether it is of a nation or an individual mind, any constitution that has beauty and religion at its centre is healthier and happier than any that is based upon vanity and materialism. That sounds childishly obvious, but "except ye become as little children," says Matthew 18:3, "ye shall not enter into the kingdom of heaven." You will probably end up in some hellish republic.

9

Drink, Drugs, and the Art of Conversation

October 2000

*C*hanging trains this summer, with two hours to kill in an unknown town, I thought I might as well have a drink. Eleven of the twelve pubs I tried were blasted by the kind of music that is properly called noise, and the twelfth was the reserve of gloomily silent drunks. What has happened to old England's hostelries? I thought, as I took my seat among the alcoholics. Where is the famous folk-art of conversation that once flourished in them? Where is the conversation itself? It has gone, I am afraid, gone the way of family dinners where children learnt how to talk properly and when to shut up. Not having acquired this art, many young people are left dumb and resentful, unable to address their seniors, to accept and respond to criticism, or even to talk sensibly among themselves. To spare them the embarrassment of speech, ear-splitting levels of noise are provided in pubs and at parties.

This applies not only to the "underclass" but to educated youths—and older people too—who are so scared of being thought "privileged" that they pander to every demonic fad, however depraved and stupid. At a country wedding I have just been to, the church service, followed by cups of tea, champagne, and gossip, proceeded as usual—until the music began, audible throughout the whole parish and drowning out the family discussions, which are largely the purpose of such events. We wished we had brought our ear trumpets.

As you get older and fleshly pleasures wane, spiritual pleasures become all the more enjoyable. Those which endure are the pleasures of good company, with good wine or narcotics, and good talk. There is no harm in drink or drugs, only in their abuse for trivial, sensual purposes that leads to alcoholism and addiction. Their true function is for the celebration of love between friends and for the development of philosophy—the love of truth. Plato at the beginning of his Laws writes at length on the proper conduct of drinking parties. These, he insists, are an essential part of education, teaching the young to keep order in their minds even when intoxicated. At these parties an older man who did not drink was appointed to direct the wild spirits of the drinkers toward high levels of thought and discourse. An example of this technique is in the Symposium, where Socrates introduces the subject of Love, allows each of the party his say, and then raises the conversation to the point of orgasm with his description of meeting Love itself.

The parties I go to are often like those that Plato wanted to reform, where everyone enjoys and admires his own blah-blah and no one listens to anyone else. We shout the other down and break into their talk. Worst of all, if an interesting subject happens to stimulate a worthwhile discussion, someone is bound to collapse it by a cheap joke or jibe. That person, I hope, will never again be me. I used to reckon that the ideal party was like one of those in Peacock's novels, where matters of art, science, and antiquarianism are debated in good humour by people of different casts of mind under the influence of a fine dinner and plenty of good wine. But Peacock was an epicurean, not a Platonist, and the subjects that now obsess me—the nature of God, true cosmology, and so on—are beyond the scope of his learned, comfortable, materialistic merry-makers.

We live in different times, and our problems are more basic and acute. That is why many of us today, lovers of good wine though we may be, find greater relevance in the illegal but readily available drugs of our age—the thought-provoking ones, cannabis, acid, ecstasy. I dare say this because we *Oldie* people have nothing to lose by speaking openly among ourselves, and we are not likely to misuse these divinely given aids to philosophy by raving under coloured lights to satanic music and thereby destroying our senses.

10
Manx Fairies

October 1998

$\mathcal{M}$y summer treat each year is to go to the geographic centre of the British Isles, halfway along the main axis from John O'Groats to the Land's End and equidistant from England, Scotland, Ireland, and Wales. That means going by ferry to the Isle of Man. The ferry ride is something I have always looked forward to—kippers for breakfast, sun and breeze on the deck, and a nap in an easy chair—and I had meant to recommend it to older readers as a perfect introduction to the peace, beauty, and simple pleasures of this most interesting island. But why do they keep changing things? The good old ferry-boat, the *King Orry* (named after the ancient and heroic Manx ruler), has been replaced by a nasty great freighter, a small part of which—noisy, cramped, and squalid—is set aside for passengers. There are no comfortable seats, just some chairs, which are impossible to sleep in, especially in rough weather when they slide about. There is everything vulgar about it that older people hate, and they would do well to avoid the experience. So you have to go to the Isle of Man by air, which is hardly in the spirit of the thing.

Though I cannot recommend the getting there, being there is delightful. One of my foibles is local transport, and if you like horse-drawn trams, electric trains, and little steam railways, the Isle of Man is where you will find them. There is no smaller island in the world with

37

its own internal rail system. Many of the stations are at national fairy glens—another unique feature. For those who like Victorian architecture and dreaming up pictures of the old days, there is a permanent exhibition of splendid seaside hotels—Balmoral, Belvoir, the Grosvenor, and so on—stretching for two miles around Douglas Bay and continuing along the coast to Port St. Mary. It is a sad show because the Isle of Man, once a romantic holiday mecca, is now completely out of fashion and its boarding houses are empty. The atmosphere is melancholy, but not unpleasantly so, and in fact, I love it—the mist, the drizzle, the solitude, and the contemplation of past glories. What more could you reasonably ask for on holiday?

At Douglas's charming Manx Museum is an exhibition about the last native Manx speakers. The very last died a few years ago, but there was a handful still around in 1948 when the Irish president, de Valera, visited Man and arranged for them to be recorded. The language died quickly, in a couple of generations, because the Manx thought that people were looking down on them for speaking it. Not wishing to be marked out as peasants, they prevented their children from learning it. With the language died the lore and traditions that belonged to it. Reality itself was changed. This was observed by several of the old survivors. Life, they said, suddenly speeded up and there wasn't time for everything any more. As one aged Manxman put it (a blacksmith who had never been beyond the borders of his own parish), "Things are so different nowadays. Why, I haven't seen any fairies for thirty years." What's going on? He might have added.

What went on was the breaking of an enchantment. From the statements of this old man and others, it is perfectly clear that fairies were once part of everyday experience, were actually seen and known. We moderns are too gross and speedy for that, but the reality to which fairies belong is more substantial than the illusion of modern life. The Manx fairies need only to bide their time and one day they will take over again. That is exactly what the Manx morals say about the crooked tax-dodgers and crooked bankers who now infest their island.

11
Nothing to Sing About

August 1994

*M*y old father used to complain about the sort of music we children liked and say that, in his day, they wrote tunes that errand boys could whistle in the streets. It was, I believe, a fashionable saying among fathers at that time. I thought it was very tedious, but now, funnily enough, I find myself saying much of the same sort of thing. One cannot, of course, expect any kind of whistling from the modern errand boys with their helmets and motorbikes, but the complaint now is that hardly anyone can whistle or sing at all. Even the Welsh, who up to a few years ago sang their hearts out in pubs and chapels, have been silenced by the forces of modernism, including the new-style police who no longer help the inspired singers homeward but persecute them with Breathalyzer tests.

Now that hardly anyone sings and music is no longer a popular art, we are at the mercy of the professionals. Come to think of it, the same thing has happened in every other department of life and culture. As individual citizens we are alienated from law, politics, economics, art, architecture, medicine, craftsmanship, and much else that was once practiced on a popular level but is now monopolised by a professional elite. How vulnerable we now are—how utterly dependent on the artificial life system, which, as even governments admit, cannot be sustained forever, or even now for much longer.

Yet we are the same people, the same God's creatures as ever, and one day we shall be able to sing and play again. My certainty on that derives from proofs given by poetic and philosophical authors that singing is an essential function of human nature and that music is the most influential of our activities. The forms of music that prevail in a society, said Plato, determine its forms of government; and the same is true of individuals. I saw that demonstrated by a youth on the street with a sound-producer clamped to his ears. His awkward gait, gestures, and grimaces exactly paralleled the ugly noise he was listening to. He needed his music, poor soul, but the professionals had betrayed him and sold him vicious trash.

Musicians generally are the most sensitive of people. Many of them, even the roughest, are somewhat aware of their responsibilities and soothe, stimulate, or assault their listeners with the very best intentions. They are of much higher quality than our modern ego-centred architects and artists, but naturally they are just as ignorant, and they are no less confused by the out-of-control state of modern life than you, I, or the government. If they knew the right note to break the spell which we have cast over ourselves, they would no doubt sound it. As it is, they can merely divert our minds from the impending shipwreck, like the orchestra on the Titanic.

In the ancient world, when the power of music was recognised, it was strictly controlled, a musical canon was established by law and musicians were not allowed to depart from it. At popular festivals the same traditional songs were heard every year, setting the tone of society and maintaining it as a harmonious unity. Something of the sort has been tried in modern totalitarian states, but dictators are vulgar people, and the bombastic type of music they favour distorts their regimes and finally destroys them. Our present cacophony is far preferable to the pompous blaring of tyrants.

I have never heard a chorus of praise to the EC or the Channel Tunnel, but there are greater ideals than these, and when we rediscover them, together with true faith, philosophy, and our own tongues, we shall then again have something worth singing about.

12

Population Control and Feng Shui, Again

February 1998

$\mathcal{T}$he cause of misanthropy, says Plato, is disappointed idealism. You begin by trusting and admiring other people, but when they display flaws or let you down you turn against them, and when the same thing keeps happening you become a confirmed misanthrope. I thought of this on reading Spike Milligan's letter in *The Oldie* last month. According to him the ills and inconveniences of modern life are mainly due to excessive population. There are "too many of us to keep up with technology." His remedy is a world-wide, five-year ban on child-bearing, with compensatory payments to young couples thus deprived of families. I know Milligan is a funny man, but his letter seemed seriously intended, and it is a good example of the misanthropy that traditionally afflicts the clown.

In one way, though, he was right. Technology does not really need ordinary people; we only get in its way. That, of course, could be seen as an argument against technology rather than people. We have been around for a long time, whereas technology is a recent upstart, so precedence should surely be given to humanity. In any case, as the astute Frenchman Jean Gimpel showed in his *End of the Future*, technology has now run its course, has nothing further of use to offer, and must

41

inevitably dwindle. Modern society is indeed dependent on it, but this, like any other dependency—on crack or heroin, say—is best fought and rejected rather than pandered to. We should therefore discourage the technomaniacs and continue as normal, honouring the biblical exhortation to be fruitful and multiply.

You need not take Milligan too seriously, but the idea of population control has serious and sinister advocates. Thomas Malthus began it in 1798 with his famous essay, which concluded that starvation of the poor was both inevitable and sanctioned by natural law. Karl Marx, getting it right for once, called him "a shameless sycophant of the ruling classes." That also applies to the most articulate and influential of the population controllers, Dr. Ehrlich of America, who is egged on and funded by big business corporations. These people are not just nasty but completely wrong in both their values and their premises. This country and the rest of the world are by no means over-peopled in comparison with former times. What has happened is that great multitudes have been sucked into cities, where they breed promiscuously, leaving wide areas of country almost deserted. That true prophet, William Cobbett, saw it for himself as he travelled around England. He found empty villages, tracts of land no longer cultivated, and great churches, built for hundreds, which had fallen to ruin for lack of congregations. This he compared with the rich, populous countryside of Catholic times. Going further back in history, he observed pre-Celtic cultivation terraces on hills where nothing had since been grown. Across southern England the mighty earthwork enclosures where craft and cattle fairs were once held bear witness to the vast numbers and wealth of the ancient Wessex people.

When Caesar invaded he was impressed by the size of the population and the farms set close together all over the country. In Ireland, the present population is but a fraction of its density before the mass emigrations, and many districts, which are now wilderness, are discovered by archaeologists to have been covered with farms and villages. Remote Scottish islands, uninhabited within living memory, have prehistoric monuments that imply the existence of several independent, highly cultured communities.

This all points to the former universality of, and the need to reinstate, that traditional code of science which the Chinese call *feng shui*. Its purpose, as stated in Abercrombie's authoritative *Town and Country Planning*, was both to preserve the beauty and harmony of the country and "to fulfil the practical purpose of supporting a dense population." I much prefer that to bribing or bullying young women into not having babies.

PART II

Albion

13

Albion,
the Spirit of the Party

May 1997

 he election is over and you all know who won, but this is written
earlier and I do not even know who I voted for. If he had a candidate in this area, it would have been for John Muir's Albion Party. A reader, Guy Reid-Brown, tipped me off about him. I read his stuff, met him, and found him entirely sound and orthodox. "Albion," he says, "was the Roman name for the whole main island of Britain, and poets have used it ever since."

"It is associated with the British landscape, imagination, and popular culture, as opposed to the establishment Britain of concentrated wealth and power. Blake gives the name Albion to his ideal, decentralised Britain where individual creativity is sovereign. What better name to give a movement of people opposed to bureaucratic misrule and lack of freedom?" Among his supporters John Muir claims bikers, pagans, and spirited people generally.

The Albion Party believes in liberation, legalisation, and the restoration of democracy through the local popular assemblies that were suppressed by the Normans. It deplores the mixture of fear and greed that impels our rulers toward the EC fortress and the rascals of Brussels, and it would like us to stop pestering the Africans with our patronising "aid." The basic idea is that which Shakespeare, Milton, Blake, Goldsmith, Cobbett, Chesterton, and all good British writers have variously expressed: to reawaken the spirit of Albion, first in ourselves and then in our institutions.

I do not think this can be done by a political party, but if John Muir wants to try it, good luck to him and my vote with it. As far as I have read and can understand, revivals of spirit come about through a process of disgust and despair, followed by yearning and prayer, and culminating in divine revelation. The key element in this process is intense desire for the ideal, which usually arises from dire necessity. The ideal is not just the satisfaction of one's own whims and appetites, but nothing less than, as St. John pictured it, the appearance of the heavenly, perfectly ordered constitution on earth, or, in William Blake's imagery, the discovery of holy Jerusalem in some mundane spot like London.

To British idealists this country is not, as the Lib-Lab-Con people pretend, a large business corporation negotiating a take-over bid, but distressed Albion, tied down and crying out for release. I cannot liberate her, nor can you or John Muir, but events are moving, slowly but surely, toward that inevitable end. A plausible date for the beginning of that movement is 1645 when the antiquarian John Aubrey, riding home after a day's hunting, passed through the village of Avebury and recognised in its great stones and earthworks the central sanctuary of an ancient British priesthood. This revelation was followed by an upsurge of mystical nationalism. William Stukeley, who sketched and surveyed the Avebury precinct for his book of 1743, while many of the stones were being demolished by local farmers, saw it as the main temple of the wise and learned druids and as evidence that divine rule on earth would first be re-established in England. His follower William Blake went further and proclaimed that the Old Testament patriarchs were druids, that Jerusalem was "the Emanation of the Giant Albion" and Britain "the Primitive Seat of the Patriarchal Religion." He was not enthusiastic about the druids, whom he criticised for restricting the spirit of Albion by a formal code of law and religion, but he agreed with Stukeley on the special, millenarian destiny of Albion's native land. This prophecy is growing ever more influential and thus more likely to be fulfilled. We must return again to the subject of Avebury, the deep mysteries concealed in it, and its unique significance in the process of awakening Albion.

14

A Lost Cause

April 1993

*M*y father was an admirer of William Cobbett and, after trying the *Rural Rides,* I became one too, reading all that I could of his books, followed by the biographies and anthologies. These include *Cobbett's Country Book* by *The Oldie'*s editor, Richard Ingrams, so I know we are on safe ground here.

Cobbett looked back to England's Golden Age before the Reformation, when a smiling countryside replete with ancestral manors and farmsteads was tended by skilled craftsmen and nurtured its large, native population in happiness and prosperity under the spell of religion. Now, before his very eyes, the old enchantment was fading away. The forces of usury were laying waste the land, upsetting the old order, and turning Merrie England into a sullen rural slum besmirched by industrial furnaces.

Cobbett's main difficulty was that he could never quite put his finger on who or what was responsible for all this. Was it bankers, Jews, Quakers, Scotsmen, greedy landlords, or something more abstract—capitalism, imperialism, materialism, modernism, Methodism, or the habit of tea-drinking? Each of these in turn he looked upon as the main enemy, but none of them quite fitted the bill, so he lumped the opposition into one conglomerate and referred to it simply as the Thing. No one since, not even among the wordy ecologists, has been able to think up a better word for it.

Nor has anyone since managed any better than Cobbett in trying to turn the tide. His most faithful disciple, H. J. Massingham, who died in 1952, poured out a vast quantity of books and articles (*The Wisdom of the Fields, The Natural Order, Where Man Belongs,* etc.) urging the necessity of reviving our traditional crafts and husbandry. The only response was from the *Country Living* types, the cottage weavers, potters, arts-and-crafts, tea-shoppe folk, who infuriated Massingham by travestying his picture of a genuine peasant revival.

Piety and common sense, twin pillars of the old order, are today's lost cause. Having gobbled up England, the Thing has expanded its appetites to the very ends of the earth, devouring every native culture. It should now be clear, even to the most nostalgic among us, that the traditional way of life and the countryside it produced will be seen no more. The bitter truth to us romantic revivalists is that there is nothing left to revive.

When renaissance comes—preceded no doubt by numerous omens and incidents of catastrophe—it will have to be very fundamental, not just a revival of old ways and customs but a new growth from the roots of culture itself. History informs us that the birth or renewal of culture is accomplished through revelation. I am not sure what that means exactly, but I think it has something to do with a vision of the true cosmic order as a model for paradise on earth. Chapter 21 of Revelation illustrates the sort of thing I have in mind.

Cobbett's vision was no doubt similar to St. John's, and he derived his assurance from it, but since his time the Thing has grown so huge and all-powerful that no-one can stand up to it. In God's good time it will burst. A graphic description of this outcome, complete with the wailings of merchant bankers, is given in Revelation 18.

Meanwhile, it is far too late to yearn for the beauties of old England restored. All that has gone. But what remains is Beauty itself, and Justice, Goodness, and the Divine Order. So now my only studies are of the numerical and musical patterns that make up the traditional cosmology. Nothing but attuning one's mind to the harmonies of revelation seems really worthwhile.

What has happened to time? Why is there now so little of it compared to the amount there used to be? ... *into those* ...

15

The Re-Conversion of England

April 1994

*T*he best literary entertainment recently has been the battle of words between RC and C-of-E journalists, reaching its climax in RC-convert Paul Johnson's ringing declaration, "We (Catholics) know how to fight." The joke began to sink in when I imagined the Brompton Oratory types under arms, marching upon St. James's Piccadilly, and I have been laughing ever since.

It was no laughing matter, of course, 400 years ago when Catholics racked and burnt alive, while Protestants hung, drew, and quartered their opposite number. Partisans on both sides have tried to rig the score in their own favour, like the Holocaust quibblers but without affecting the overall result, that the atrocities discredited the Church generally, and the British have ever since been skeptical toward religious fanaticism and ecclesiastical dogma. That is how we shaped our amiable Church of England, unpretentious, ignorant of the Mysteries, well-meaning, honestly confused.

The bloody, barbaric iconoclasm of the Protestant Reformation destroyed the religious, social fabric of old England and opened the way to materialism. That presumably was God's will, meaning we must have deserved it, and since there is no going back, that is the end of the matter. I sympathise with the Catholics' ideal of the Re-conversion of England, by which they mean the Holy Grail restored, but it seems unlikely that the substitution of one Church for another would achieve that result.

Look at Italy, for example. There is great power in the Catholics' appeal on behalf of the Old Church, but not so much when they identify it with their own. Our native Church was Celtic, which owed nothing to Rome and seems to have been a reformation of Druidism directed by missionaries from the Holy Land.

We never really took to St. Augustine. He arrived in Canterbury in 597, telling us that we should be more zealous in converting the remaining pagans and that we should acknowledge the central authority of Rome. This appealed to Europhiles and to ambitious clerics such as St. Wilfrid, through whom the Roman Church finally prevailed.

St. Augustine himself had a rough ride on his mission. At Cerne Abbas in Dorset they tied fish tails to his coat, evidently a traditional sign of disapproval, and in Wales he was more seriously rebuffed. When summoned to meet him, the Welsh bishops took council together and decided that if he stood up to greet them they would go along with him. But Augustine remained seated when they entered the council chamber, so they politely told him they would rather retain their own ancient, Celtic form of Christianity.

The Celtic Church was tolerant even of good pagans, and, as far as is known, created no martyrs. There was no agonizing about female ministers. As under the Druid system, women were qualified to inherit property, lead tribes, and preside over religious houses. They were also preachers, prophets, hermits, healers, following their natural talents.

Both our Catholics and our Protestants proclaim themselves heirs of the native spiritual tradition and I cannot easily decide which of them is most justified. So I am resigned to remaining as I happen to be, a sort of inert Anglican, knowing nothing, having no key to the Mysteries, but wedded to the dear spirit of this country and its dear though desperately infuriating inhabitants.

16
Anglo-Saxon Attitudes

December 1992

*T*alking the other day to an Anglo-Saxon revivalist, I thought, how sensible this person is, and how right. I have met several of the kind before and they always come round to complaining about something they call the Norman Yoke. This, they say, is still upon us and it means that we have had no proper form of democracy for over 900 years, ever since King Harold fought one battle too many.

This, apparently, is how it used to work in the old Saxon days. Every village, hamlet, and farmstead had its moot, *gemot, raad, ting,* or council, which every free man was expected to attend. They organised the village economy, the apportioning of land, the division of labour, the maintenance of roads and ditches, and so on, and they gave judgement about local disputes and grievances. More serious cases and appeals to higher authority were referred to the hundred court, which was made up of deputies elected from each of the local bodies. The hundreds in turn sent representatives to the shire court, and from the shires were drawn the members of the regional assemblies in Wessex, Mercia, Northumbria, or whatever else was going on at the time. Above these, whenever anyone could organise it, was the national council, the *witenagemot,* which every freeman of England had a right to attend.

This assembly had several important functions. It was the supreme court of law, it proposed and ratified legislation and, above all, it elected or confirmed the succession of the king. It also, if necessary, deposed him. In those days there was no sentimentality about "royal families." If the king didn't work, if he lost all his battles and was unable to make it stop or start raining, they got rid of him. It was not always easy, of course, but that was the theory of it.

The attractive thing about this system was that everyone knew whom they were voting for. There was no question of campaigns, with lies and drivel from odd-looking creatures one has never before seen or heard of. No one had a "public image" or stood or ran for anything. From the village level all the way up, deputies to higher councils were nominated by their peers, who knew them very well and could recognise whether they were qualified to represent the common interest. "That," said my Anglo-Saxon revivalist friend, "is what I call real democracy."

All these assemblies, even the national council, met in the open air. This was something the Druids had always insisted upon, and even the Norman Yoke did not entirely obliterate the custom. They were always held at some traditional spot—an ancient mound, stone, tree, or cross-roads, and often, as at Runnymede, on an islet in a lake or river. On the days of assembly these places were held sacred and everyone could speak freely under religious protection.

William the Conqueror and his Frenchified hangers-on grabbed all the lands and offices in England and gave them to feudal landlords protected by centralised government. The local moots lost most of their powers and were dragged off their islands and tumuli to sit within the castle walls under the eye of the lord. In several recorded cases, people complaining about this said that at indoor meetings they felt liable to be bewitched. This seems to put it rather well. There is certainly a great deal of witchery involved in modern election campaigns. Who knows what these people are up to? Perhaps we should return to the old Anglo-Saxon way of conducting public affairs—publicly, democratically, and in the open air.

17
Brassy Britain

March 1999

I know you cannot always believe what you read in the papers but they can hardly have made up Mr. Hague's New Year speech where he expressed his ideal vision of Britain. He said that he wants us to be "urban, ambitious, sporty, fashion-conscious, multi-ethnic, brassy, self-confident, and international." Really! Does he think we are a bunch of Spice Girls? Are we not loud and vulgar enough already? Does this stuff really come from the leader of a party called Conservative? It sounds to me like a kind of low-grade fascism.

I recognise that Mr. Hague is just pandering and that they all do it, but it is cruel to mislead people like that. Everyone wants to be happy, and most people soon come to realise that if you make yourself ugly, selfish, and aggressive you have no chance of being so. Teenagers like to flirt with truculence, but they drop it when they see that it is not attracting lovers. Happiness has some essential ingredients, first among which are acceptance of life as it is and a high level of interest in it. If you can underpin that by cultivating awe and admiration for the Creator of this miracle and celebrating the cause of your existence, then there is no reason (give or take the occasional mishap or holocaust) to be bored, lonely, sick, or miserable. In competition with Hague I offer this vision of our country, Albion, in its natural state of happiness. It is not urban in its values but rural, based on the essential facts of life; it is not ambitious but contented; it is not "sporty," which is a flashy word, but sporting and high-spirited. Nor is it fashion-conscious. That is all very well for schoolgirls; they cannot help it. But no one of any consequence pays attention to fads and fashions. And, of course, it is not "brassy and self-confident" but quietly at ease with itself.

What about "multi-ethnic"? That is the present state of Albion, at least in its urban parts, and it is not necessarily a bad thing. But it is not self-evidently a good thing either, and the same goes for all the other mixings and levellings—of caste, class, rank, and culture and between the sexes—that are identified without question as signs of progress toward virtue. So they would be, if virtue lay in the direction of uniformity, with each of us reduced to a mere unit of humanity. That may be what governments want, and it is openly desired by the world powers of finance and propaganda. But the trouble is that when all social distinctions are lost and everyone operates on the same level, everyone competes for those marks of distinction that remain, which are not virtue but fame and money. That is why the man wants us to be brassy.

Dear old John Major was honest and simple enough to paint his own pretty picture of how England ought to be. He babbled amiably of sleepy villages, polite manners, proper old-fashioned vicars, and the novels of Jane Austen, and one can hardly be cruel about that. One can, however, do better. Behind such personal daydreams is the ideal, universal dream of paradise on earth. These days we are suspicious of idealism, and for good reason. The century now passing has been an age of dictatorships and tyrannies, producing more mass misery than has been known in any previous era. All these have been characterised by atheism, idolatry, and the pursuit of man-made utopias. This is false idealism, the exact opposite of the real thing, of that pre-existing "pattern in the heavens," which Plato urged his students to study and establish in their hearts. His reference was to the numerically based traditional code of cosmology, which is revealed from time to time and enters human consciousness, providing the model for true civilisation, long lasting and divinely ordered. I wish now that I had started with this subject and not been distracted by Mr. Hague's nonsense.

18

The Centre of Britain

August 1992

If you hate the EC and want to remove yourself from its jurisdiction while remaining in the British Isles, the one thing you can do is become a resident in the Isle of Man. It is an old-fashioned Celtic realm, extremely pretty, riddled with fairy glens and unexplored antiquities, and it has the best national railway system in the world. If you do not mind a one-party state, if you stay out of politics and avoid the attentions of the Manx mafia, you could live there very happily. And I believe there are certain tax advantages.

Before the Norwegians and their meddlesome Vikings took over in the tenth century, the tribes of Man were ruled by a Celtic high king who held court at the exact central point. There the original Tynwald was held. The present site at St. John's where the Manx parliament meets every Midsummer Day upon an earthen mound in the open air is not more than 1,000 years old. It is a Norse innovation; yet so transitory are human affairs that the St. John's Tynwald claims to be the oldest continuous legislative assembly in the world. So the only example of a 1,000-year Reich is the Isle of Man.

There is a Governor of Man, appointed by the Queen, but his powers have largely been usurped by the democratically elected House of Keys, whose twenty-four members debate local affairs in a panelled chamber with a bewigged Mr. Speaker. They are the visible tip of the Manx mafia and are united by their determination to rid the island of sex and drugs.

One could easily smoke a joint in a deserted third-class compartment of the Douglas to Port Erin steam train or on the incredibly picturesque electric railway through Laxey to Ramsey. Sexual activity is far more rigidly policed. The Manx custom of birching delinquents has recently been given up, but it was only this year that the laws against homosexuality were repealed—by a majority of one in the House of Keys. This was only achieved through persistent bullying from Whitehall. The British have no right to interfere with the internal affairs of Man, but in this case, claimed the Home Office, they were acting upon the order of their bosses, the European Human rights people, who had insisted upon the change.

So Manx independence is not quite what it seems on paper. The only constitutional link with Britain is that Queen Elizabeth has inherited the rights of the old high king as Lord of Man. It issues its own delightful stamps and coins and runs its own national institutions. Yet if the Europeans disapprove of any detail in the Manx polity, they instruct the British to intervene—and so far the Manx have caved in. If I were in the Manx mafia I would insist upon real independence. This could simply be gained by the Manx abolishing their monarchy, thus cutting out the Queen. They could then choose a new high king, install him in a Manx-language ceremony at Keeil Abban, the pre-Norse Tynwald centre, and restore whatever floggings, birchings, and other ancient customs they thought appropriate. Brussels no doubt would order the British government to send a task force and re-enact the Falklands campaign more conveniently in Douglas Bay. On the other hand, a UDI would do wonders for the flagging Manx tourist industry.

If you like beautiful scenery and sweet-tempered natives you should go to the Isle of Man. It is not at all remote but lies at the exact centre of the British Isles, less than fifty miles from England, Scotland, Ireland, and Wales, and precisely on the line from Land's End to John O'Groats.

19

Citizens of Stonehenge

July 1992

*T*he Stonehenge convoy, New Age travellers or whatever they are now called, are surely the most useful people in this country, because they constantly remind us of our rightful heritage, the Merrie England, which we lost at the bloody Reformation. Until then, since prehistoric times there had been perpetual feasts and festivals all over the land and the roads between them had thronged with pilgrims, pedlars, and party-goers. Under our native laws, codified in about 450 BC by King Molmutius, the roads between sanctuaries were themselves sacred, and travellers upon them had no fear of being molested.

Anthony Burgess has recently described the modern travellers as "pilgrims without a shrine." But they do have a shrine—Stonehenge. It actually belongs to them as part of the British nation to whom, in 1918, it was presented by locksmith Mr. Cecil Chubb. He had purchased it at auction for £6,000. Attached to his gift were certain conditions: that the public be allowed access to the stones and that no further buildings be erected on the site. All his conditions have been flouted by the nation's trustees, English Heritage, whose Ceaucescu-style additions—the razor-wire barriers, concrete tunnel, coach park, and trinket shops—have made it into one of Europe's most repulsive tourist attractions.

The people around Stonehenge have always enjoyed the right of assembling there at midsummer to greet the sun as it rises in line with the axis. Early this century they were joined by the reconstituted Order of Druids, and in 1974 the martyr Wally Hope (mysteriously deceased) renewed ancient custom with his Stonehenge People's Festival. This grew over the next ten years as travellers instinctively began to imitate their ancestors and gather at their national temple for free-spirited solstice ceremonies. During this period the stones were quite undamaged and the festival camped harmlessly on land that had long been ravaged by deep-ploughing farmers, army tanks, and archaeologists' spades.

Suddenly in 1985 English Heritage announced a total ban on the festival. A five-mile exclusion zone was set around Stonehenge, and when a party of defiant traditionalists attempted to proceed as usual, the police violently arrested them, beating men, women, and children alike and smashing up their vehicles. This one-sided affair was called the Battle of the Beanfield. Every midsummer at Stonehenge has since been marked by officious brutalities. The druids are excluded from their temple and the only witnesses of the unique sunrise are regiments of police and some foreign journalists. They are all said to be Freemasons.

The anarchic Stonehenge Festival brought peace to this country, repeating the ancient formula for social harmony. Before modern ignorance set in it was the custom everywhere to invoke the Lord of Misrule for a season. During his brief reign the laws were suspended or reversed. People danced, drank, and, presumably, took whatever drugs their humble hedgerows provided. Then, having mocked and ignored the normal restrictions of their social order, they lived more contentedly within it for the rest of the year. The principle is well illustrated today by the Notting Hill Carnival. English Heritage plans monumental developments at Stonehenge for the degrading purpose of cramming in even more tourists. They should do us all a favour by restoring it to its original use as a universal temple and midsummer place of festival.

20

Sacred Monarchy

September 1992

*T*he weakest and most vulnerable of our national institutions is surely the "royal family." There is nothing special about the Queen's relatives. No one has anointed or crowned them or conferred spiritual powers upon them. Nor do they seem necessary. We do not hear of any "papal family," supported by the Vatican and consisting of His Holiness's random aunts and cousins. Even the Holy Family contained only three members.

The comparison between the British monarch and the Pope is appropriate because they are both spiritual rather than secular rulers. As Defender of the Faith and head of the national Church, the Queen is bound to uphold the State Cult, which is not merely the Protestant foundation of that bloody old proto-Stalin, Henry VIII, but harks back to far earlier times and is rooted in the mystery of sacred kingship. At her Coronation she became the receptacle of the collective national spirit and thus refers to herself as We. She also acquired the power of healing scrofula by means of the Royal Touch, a prerogative which has not in fact been exercised since the time of Queen Anne.

Having a soft spot for the British Israelites, though disliking their present mood of truculent nationalism, I read and enjoy their literature about our identity with the Ten Lost Tribes. According to the BIs, the

Queen is titular heir to Melchizadek, the priest-king of ancient Israel. One of their evidences is the Coronation Stone, clamped beneath the seat of the Coronation Chair in Westminster Abbey. Since 1296, when Edward I took the stone from the Scots, every English monarch has been crowned upon it. Even Cromwell used it for his installation as Lord Protector. Before the Scots had it, it is said to have been for about a thousand years the coronation stone of the Irish kings at Tara, and previous to that it was "Jacob's pillow," the stone which he set up at Bethel. These may not be historical facts, but the legend is so powerful that, had the Scottish raiders who stole the Stone in 1950, just before the last Coronation, not returned it in time, Elizabeth II could not have been properly installed.

Another evidence is the Crown of St. Edward, which is placed on the sovereign's head at the most solemn moment of the crowning ceremony. It is only a replica but it faithfully imitates the ancient original, destroyed in the time of Cromwell. Around its rim are twelve different gemstones, the same as those that ornamented the New Jerusalem in Revelation and formed the breastplate of Israel's High Priest. Like the tribes of Israel or types of mankind, which they symbolise, the twelve jewels are separated into four groups of three, with each group placed beneath a larger stone. At the top of the Crown, below a jeweled cross, is a golden orb representing the perfected earth under divine governance. Through these and other symbols activated at her coronation, the Queen received her rights and responsibilities from the supreme source of authority. The "royal family," born or unborn, were quite untouched by this process and are just ordinary citizens who happen to be related to a sour little woman called Elizabeth Windsor.

Those readers with understanding will recognise that all this nonsense is perfectly true and that our divinely authorised Queen should be encouraged to fulfill what she knows to be her sworn duty, to use the powers invested in her for invoking God's kingdom upon earth and restoring this country to its natural state as a terrestrial paradise.

21
Taking the St. Michael

March 2000

A delightful feature of these present times is that they are times of revelations. A revelation is something that comes into your mind when you feel the need for it and are looking for it, even though you may not know quite what you are looking for. My own experiences of this range from the "library-angel" effect known to all writers, whereby the unique book or item of knowledge that you need coincidentally turns up, to the full-blown vision of the Heavenly Jerusalem, just as it appeared to St. John.

A revelation that occurred to me over thirty years ago is the St. Michael line through the extreme width of southern England. It had long been a secret, forgotten by everyone, but once recognised it stirred up old memories and shed light on one of the deepest mysteries in ancient British history.

Traditionally, our history begins in the Bronze Age with the invasion of Brutus the Trojan, whose extensive dynasty ruled the whole island up to Christian times. One of these kings, Belinus, built four great stone highways running straight between the extremities of the country. They were regarded as linear sanctuaries where all could travel safely. Parts of these ancient roads survive as tracks or modern roads, but for the most part their lines are lost and scholars have always disputed about their routes and names. One that is not disputed is the Icknield Way, related by name to the Iceni tribe of East Anglia. Traces of it are aligned between the eastern end of Suffolk and Avebury in Wiltshire, the ritual centre of ancient England—and where there are not traces, the line remains audible in the "ick" names of villages upon it: Ickworth, Ixworth, Rickinghall, Dickleburgh, and so on. Projected west of Avebury, the same line goes directly to the Land's End of Cornwall, thus linking the two most distant extremities of southern Britain and forming its axis.

West of Avebury the "ick" sound is heard in the archangel Mikhael, familiarly called St. Michael, whose sanctuaries are ranged along the old way. The first thing that drew my attention to this axis was the fact that Glastonbury Tor and another island-hill, Burrowbridge Mump, both topped by ruined churches to St. Michael, stand upon it in line with Avebury, with signs of a former pilgrims' path between them. Further west other St. Michael sites, characteristically placed like St. Michael's Mount on rocky heights, occur on or beside the axis line, which continues over the last holy hill of Cornwall, St. Michael's, Carn Brae, to a spot near the Land's End.

This surely marks the line of the prehistoric way, which, according to certain antiquarian writers, did indeed follow the axis from the East Anglian coast to the tip of Cornwall, with the Avebury temple its centrepoint. But why should Belinus or anyone else have constructed such a way? Its traditions indicate that it was a sacred path used by pilgrims and festival-goers to Avebury and other shrines. Folklore identifies it as the path by which Jesus came from Cornwall to Glastonbury. It is a mystery still, but it is not without comparison or context.

Further researches have shown that in every country where revelation has occurred and where societies have been formed after the ideal model of the cosmos, the dominant symbol is the pole of the universe, represented by the main geographical axis through that country. Upon it—ideally at its midpoint—was located the national sanctuary. A clear-cut example of this is in mainland Shetland, where the central administration and law court was situated on an islet in a loch, precisely halfway along the main north-south axis of the forty-five-mile-long island.

The St. Michael line is clearly such an axis, and it tells that here in ancient times was a national, cosmologically based social order, such as William Blake dreamt of. Revelations are flowing and there are more to come. That is why I cannot sustain pessimism about the future.

22
A Musical Enchantment

July 2001

*I*f you are not properly educated it is difficult to develop interests and enjoy life. So it is a shame that many children leave school with no interest in anything they were made to learn. If only they could be introduced to the Mysteries and Enchantments of Britain. Some of them may not readily be enthused by this subject. But unless there is some defect in your imagination you cannot help being excited by the modern discoveries that have completely changed our outlook on ancient history and culture. An example of what I am talking about is that vast relic of archaic priestcraft called the Circle of Perpetual Choirs.

The institution of perpetual choirs was taken over by our early Christians from the Druids. In monasteries all over the country a ceaseless round of chanting was maintained day and night by teams of choristers. There were never fewer than twelve of them, corresponding to the twelve notes of the chromatic scale, but in some monasteries there were said to be thousands of singers. The purpose of the chant was to hold the country under the "enchantment" of a musical cycle that varied with the times and seasons and set the tone for the music at popular festivals. That is the meaning of the old tradition that government was originally by music alone.

A Welsh bardic triad names three of the great British choirs. They were at Stonehenge, Glastonbury, and a site in south Wales near Llantwit Major where St. Illtyd had his monastic college. These places are the same distance one from another, and the angles between them are of 144 degrees. This angle at Stonehenge coincides with the Avenue toward midsummer sunrise and locates the next choir site at Goring-on-Thames (Gor meaning "choir," as in Bangor). One hundred forty-four degrees is the angle of a ten-sided polygon, implying that there were originally ten choirs around the circumference of a large circle.

The distance between each of the choirs is 38.4 statute miles, or 40 ancient Greek miles, so the calculated radius of the circle is 64.8 Greek miles. That measure has great significance to metrologists. In the earth's meridian there are 25,920 or 64.8 × 400 Greek miles, so the distance from each of the perpetual choir sites to the centre of the circle is a 400th part of the distance round the earth, measured through the poles.

The centre of this remarkable circle is in the Malvern hills, at the spot where three counties meet—Herefordshire, Worcestershire, and Gloucestershire. Once it was marked by a legendary tree called the White-leafed Oak. Local people used it for telling fortunes and, according to a local author, it was "unquestionably of Druidic origin." By strange coincidence the three cathedral cities whose counties meet at the centrepoint of the Perpetual Choirs circle now maintain the famous Three Choirs Festival.

You cannot easily date this vast ancient structure. It must predate Stonehenge, where evidence of building begins in the sixth millennium BC. One thing it shows is that the network of prehistoric monuments and sanctuaries was largely designed at one time and for one great purpose. To prove that for yourself begin at the former chapel of "St. Michael at Gare Hill" on the Wilts-Somerset border, precisely located on the Glastonbury Abbey–Stonehenge line, 18 Greek miles from the first, 22 from the second. This now-forgotten hilltop sanctuary determined the northern line of the Stonehenge Cursus, which is oriented upon it, and also the location of Woodhenge, on the same line and exactly 24 Greek miles from Gare Hill. These researches take you far more deeply into the mysteries of antiquity than archaeologists have ever reached. They illuminate those times when the power of music and custom were so effective that people lived happily and did not even know there was a government.

23

A Dream of Old Tracks

September 1993

Sometimes I have a dream of England as it was, or should have been, a dream of the Golden Age in terms of different periods. Its earliest setting is the Bronze Age, when nobles were noble, the peasants highly cultured under the spell of Druid bardistry, and the scholars and craftsmen more refined than ever before or since. Another scene is in the Middle Ages, before the Reformation knocked the spirit out of Merrie England. The rural economy is at its zenith, the village folk are skilful and pious, there is a constant round of festivals, and harmony is maintained through the perpetual chanting of monkish choristers.

The most stirring of these dreams is intensified by the nostalgia which attaches itself to the recent past, just before one's own period. It is set in the brief heyday of railways, before the motoring craze caught on. The dream landscape is in, perhaps, East Anglia at midsummer. Under a shimmering heat-haze the countryside is still and ageless, and at a little branch-line station we drowsily await the engine which is taking us from one village to another. A whistle is heard, there is a puff of smoke, a green flag is waved, and we are rattling busily through ripe cornfields. At the junction, where we change for the local market town, countrywomen with baskets of farm produce come on board, with a travelling salesman, an antiquarian tourist, a party of schoolchildren all familiar and in order.

The reformation which ended this dream happened in 1963, when Dr. Beeching's axe fell upon branch-lines and even certain main-line routes. County towns and cathedral cities, like Wells in Somerset, could no longer be reached by rail. From then on one could hardly travel the country except in a car. This, so I thought at the time, was a plot on behalf of the oil industry. More likely it was an offering to the dominant god of Progress. It destroyed the remains of the old economy and delivered us irrevocably into the hands of big business.

Others must have had my railway dream, for many people have dedicated themselves to making it real again, forming groups and restoring train services to rambling cross-country routes of yesteryear. In defiance of secular economics and directly against government policy, they have followed the guidance of their dream and, in many cases, have made it come true. If only our rulers would learn from that lesson, to dream before acting, to consider the ideal and, where necessary, compromise with it rather than constantly pandering to the low-level reality of materialism.

Having business in Kingswear, Devon, I took the train there and found that the last lap, from Paignton onward, was on the rails of a local steam preservation society. Everything was normal in an old-fashioned way: cardboard tickets, a waiting-room with tea, a poorly sprung wooden carriage on a standard-gauge line. Yet on this private railway my fellow passengers were ecstatic. They laughed, exclaimed, gazed rapturously out of the window, behaving quite differently from the normal run of British Rail "customers." At first I wondered if they had spiked the tea, but then I saw the influence of a dream, dreamt by the line's proprietors and gratefully accepted by the good folk who paid money for their trip. As Colin Wilson keeps reminding us, you experience life with the intensity that you bring to it. So now I treat every train journey as if it were on a line that some dreamer had lovingly restored. In that way you can enjoy the exquisite pleasures of nostalgia, not for the imagined past but for something which is actually happening.

24
When Jesus Came to England

July 1996

Jerusalem
By William Blake

And did those feet in ancient time
Walk upon England's mountains green:
And was the holy Lamb of God,
On England's pleasant pastures seen?

And did the Countenance Divine,
Shine forth upon our clouded hills?
And was Jerusalem builded here,
Among these dark Satanic Mills?

Bring me my Bow of burning gold:
Bring me my arrows of desire:
Bring me my Spear: O clouds unfold!
Bring me my Chariot of fire!

I will not cease from Mental Fight,
Nor shall my sword sleep in my hand:
Till we have built Jerusalem,
In England's green & pleasant Land.

$\mathcal{S}$ ome wretched clergyman has been objecting to William Blake's verses (taken from the preface to his [epic poem] *Milton*), which makes up the hymn "Jerusalem." He says they are patronizing, a chauvinistic delusion, and whatnot, and he is embarrassed by the notion that "those feet" ever walked upon England's mountains green. I had never before given much thought to the old story of Jesus coming to England, but the dispirited, whingeing tone of this complaint inclined me to a passionate belief in it. So I researched the subject and found, as expected, that there is plenty of impeccable evidence to justify Blake's insight.

The historical record of Jesus in England begins with the early annals of the Celtic Church. St. David in the sixth century acknowledged that Jesus himself had dedicated the church at Glastonbury to his Mother, and a similar story, though with Jesus actually building the church, is repeated in a tenth-century life of St. Dunstan. The most reputable of early British chroniclers, Gildas, in the fourth century asserted that Christianity was established in England by AD 37, and this was recognised in the early Church councils, where the English bishops were given priority due to the antiquity of their foundation.

There is far more genuine folklore about Jesus's presence in England than can be found in the Holy Land. The story it tells is that during his "lost years," before beginning his mission at the age of thirty, Jesus came here to be initiated by the Druids. That would not be surprising, since classical authors record that the Druids of that time practiced the deepest Mysteries and that foreign nobles sent their children to the British colleges.

He was brought to Cornwall by his uncle, Joseph of Arimathea, a merchant, who bartered Mediterranean goods (the Druids never accepted money) for the West Britons' tin. They then proceeded eastward to Glastonbury where they traded lead and other minerals with the miners of the Mendip Hills. After the Crucifixion St. Joseph returned to Glastonbury bearing the mystic "cruets" associated with the Holy Grail, and settled as one of twelve ritualistic choristers on the site later revered as "the holiest ground in England."

Nineteenth-century folklorists, Baring-Gould and others, collected numerous stories from the miners of west Cornwall and the Mendips, which testified to an ancient belief that Jesus had been among them. Items of Somerset lore suggest that he and Uncle Joseph trod the ancient sacred path between hilltop sanctuaries, now dedicated to St. Michael, which stretches from Land's End through Glastonbury Tor and the Stone Age temple of Avebury to the furthest extremity of eastern England.

Having justified my emotional belief in Jesus coming to England, I then gave it up. When people insist the legend is true I remind them that there is no actual proof of it. On the other hand, when scoffers denigrate it I vigorously defend its probability. As a philosopher you have to be ruthlessly perverse.

The point of the story is not so much in the past as in its implications for the future. In his long, prophetic poem *Jerusalem,* Blake described the primordial English paradise where Druid priests upheld the true, simple religion that Jesus tried to restore. Their influence spread throughout the world and gave rise to the Jewish and other religions. Then came the Fall, corruption set in, the priests began sacrificing, and their rule thereafter was through fear. Thus the human mind no longer dwells in a spiritual Eden but in the low realm of materialistic delusion. The native English prophecy, as Blake powerfully restated it, is that upon this beautiful land will descend again the heavenly Jerusalem.

That prophecy is inescapable and it answers all the questions that bother us today—such as Britain's role in Europe and the EC. Our destiny is to be the Holy Land of Europe. It is a big responsibility, but no one else wants to take it on, and it is not the sort of thing you can leave to the Belgians.

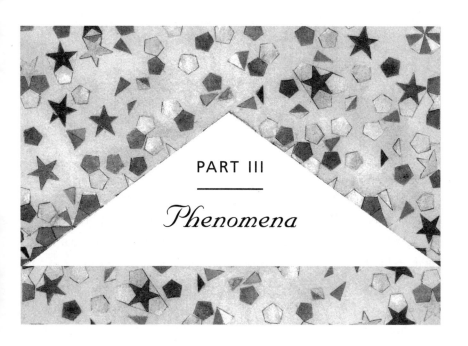

PART III

Phenomena

25

Abductions

August 1995

*T*hey say that poor old John Mack is being persecuted, and I am really not surprised. He is a professor at Harvard University, a psychiatrist, and a Pulitzer Prize winner for his book on Lawrence of Arabia. That is all very well, but everyone has a weak spot, and with Mack it is alien abductions. He studies and counsels people who have been abducted by creatures from other planets or dimensions, and he has written a book on the subject, which has become an American bestseller. No wonder his colleagues are jealous. Now they are trying to drive him out of Harvard on the grounds that he is discrediting them with his nonsense.

Alien abductions are a big thing today, especially in America—though the first victim I ever met was a Belfast lad who had been shockingly molested by spacewomen. That was in 1968, and since then the phenomenon has spread so widely as now to be almost commonplace. I have since met a great many abductees, most of them women who have been traumatised by an experience, which they interpret as rape by alien entities. They even have support groups where they meet and discuss their predicaments. Like John Mack I am impressed by their sincerity and the genuineness of their suffering, but I cannot follow him to his literal conclusion, that actual beings from other worlds are responsible for it all. That is the popular line, beloved by the great American UFO public, and Mack is not alone in peddling it. Another professor, David Jacobs, preaches the doctrine of extra-terrestrial penetration, and he also has become a bestseller.

If you meet these learned specialists and want to make them angry, just mention the word "folklore." To Americans of that sort, folklore is something that happened in the olden days when people were simple and gullible. They would imagine that they had been kidnapped by fairies or that their baby had been exchanged for a wizened elf. They never mentioned spacecraft or alien invaders. Abductions nowadays are described in space-age imagery, and that is why the professors think that they must alert the world to the Coming of Space Rapists.

The difficulty I have in talking about such things is that the modern mind has become so limited and single-visioned that it has lost touch with normal perception. For every phenomenon it demands a physical explanation, no matter how fantastic. Normal minds in all ages have accepted the realm of mystery, the irrational side of existence, and the monstrous phantoms that regularly arise from it. Yetis, dragons, and lake monsters belong to that "daimonic reality," as Patrick Harpur has called it, and similarly daimonic are the nasty creatures that abduct or violate people and disturb their minds. You can sell a lot of books by identifying them as spacemen, but properly they are called "demons."

The proof that modern abductions are repetitions of an ancient pattern is that in every case, from mythology and folklore to today's UFO literature, the person who undergoes contact with otherworldly beings is mentally changed by the experience. Some minds are destroyed by it, but in many cases the effect is like that of an initiation process. The professors are quite right to be interested in what is happening, but they too are victims of the modern mind, and with their theories of space-aliens they are sadly short-sighted. It is no wonder that demonic forces are becoming rife among us, and it is nothing to worry about. Nature works through the mind and brings the appropriate influence at each season. The daemons we experience are precisely those that we deserve and need.

26

UFO Abductions
and the End of Innocence

October 1993

*T*he first UFO contactee I met was a young lad from a poor Protestant family in Northern Ireland, named Ivor Brown. One evening he was walking along a dark country road toward a dance hall when he saw in front of him an oval-shaped object. Some creatures came out of it and took him inside, where he was seduced or whatever you call it by two strange but attractive females. Somehow Ivor got in touch with Desmond Leslie, the author of the very first UFO book, who took me to meet him.

We were inexperienced at that time, so were rather disconcerted by Ivor Brown. Our main concern was whether or not he was lying, and our ideas on how to tell a liar from an honest man were unimaginatively conventional. We had hoped to find the type of reliable witness who appeals to lawyers, firm-eyed and rational-minded. That was not Ivor Brown. He was nervous, impressionable, uneducated, and prone to symptoms that are familiar to psychiatrists. Ever since his experience he had maintained psychic contact with his abductors and knew when they were near his house. His sensitivity spread to the rest of the family. Their minds and habits were changed and they left their home to go on psychically guided travels. The last I saw of Ivor was when he passed through London with old Mr. Brown and a younger brother, on their way to visit the grave of Matthew Hopkins, the fanatical witch-finder of seventeenth-century Suffolk.

There is now a vast literature on the subject of "UFO abductions"— the modern folklore term for the kind of experience described by Ivor Brown. A large and growing number of similar encounters are reported all over the world, particularly in America. Opinions are divided about their meaning. Some say that they are to do with extra-terrestrial beings, while others believe they have a psychological origin. My own persuasion is that the sensible approach to the phenomenon of UFO abductees is by comparing it with past records—the records of folklore.

In any regional account of British folklore one can find stories about people who have been abducted by unworldly creatures, conventionally identified as fairies. The details in such cases are infinitely varied, but one detail is always the same. In every account of an abduction, whether by fairies, demons, or UFO-creatures, the abductee is mentally changed and acquires a new, spiritual perception. The results are not always of obvious benefit—abductees are likely to become lonely, melancholy, introspective. Some are persuaded that they have gone mad and there are always a few who think that God or the Venusians have chosen them to reform mankind.

In certain cases, however, a person who has undergone the abduction experience is awakened to life and gains the level of understanding, which, in ancient and tribal societies, was induced by a ritual initiation.

I now know that Ivor Brown was telling the truth, that he had a genuine, traumatic experience and that he naturally described it in modern, space-age imagery rather than, as he would have done a generation or so earlier, in terms of demons and fairies. The actual cause of that experience is a mystery, which, I feel sure, will never finally be explained. Yet is has to be accepted as a real, effective phenomenon. To any sympathetic reader who has the slightest idea what I am driving at,

I offer for contemplation the following suggested connections: violation of innocence by "UFO abductors"; by rumoured covens of "cult ritualists"; by tribal elders in the course of their initiation of adolescents. These are terrible things to undergo, but the victim may find certain compensations, such as maturity and a finer sensibility.

27
Bogus Social Workers

April 1992

*R*eaders who have nothing better to do than leaf through their local newspapers are asked to keep an eye out for reports of BSW sightings.

Over the past three years hundreds of Bogus Social Workers have been observed all over Britain, mostly in the poor districts of former industrial towns in the North. The majority of them are women, single or in pairs, aged about thirty, well dressed, smartly made up, with educated, non-local accents. The occasional male BSW is similarly official looking. Both sexes carry briefcases and clipboards. They say they have come to inspect your children. Sometimes they want to take them away, but they have never actually done so, and they have rarely been known to touch or examine a child. When you challenge their credentials or threaten to call the police, they make excuses and leave.

At the peak of the first great BSW outbreak, in the summer of 1990, the police were investigating over 250 cases in what was described as Britain's biggest-ever manhunt. Urged on by lubricious journalists (the *News of the World* offered a £10,000 reward for the capture of a BSW) they set up a headquarters in Sheffield and issued descriptions of the BSW types they were seeking to "interview." The only effect of this was to multiply the number of reported incidents. Not one of the unlicensed baby-inspectors was ever arrested and the *News of the World* prize is still waiting to be claimed.

The police, who spend much of their time chasing phantoms, are fairly experienced in the world of intermediate reality. It did not take them long to realise that the BSWs were not, as was first supposed, gangs of paedophiles or Satanists but a new type of thought-form, similar in kind to the Men in Black (MIBs) who are often sighted during outbreaks of UFO-type phenomena. Most of the BSW reports, said a police spokesman, were cases of mistaken identity or products of the hysteria about child molestation whipped up by press and television.

Not surprisingly, the first wave of BSW sightings came soon after the Cleveland affair, when busloads of children were taken into care, and their parents and uncles were accused of abusing them. Nor is it surprising that Cleveland erupted a year after the importation of a deadly virus from America—the virus of witch-hunting. This plague has been endemic in the United States since the earliest days, but the new version, which emerged in the early 1980s, was particularly virulent. Communities were gripped by the notion that covens of satanic ritualists were active among them, kidnapping babies and sacrificing them in obscene ceremonies.

Rosie Waterhouse, whose fine article (she never writes any other kind) ornamented the first issue of *The Oldie,* has described how in 1988 this nonsense spread to Britain. One of its side effects is the creation of sinister thought-forms such as BSWs. Thought-forms are indicators of psychological disturbance, and there are similarities between the present outbreak and a well-known psychosis that has afflicted Europe intermittently since the Middle Ages. It is but a short step from believing that unknown Satanists are devouring Christian babies to reviving the murderous "blood libel," which attributed such activities to the Jews. Those who give credence to satanic rumours should understand the nature of the thought-forms they are encouraging.

Proof that our brilliant police force recognises the power of thought-forms is given by Mr. Dan Crompton, Chief Constable of Nottinghamshire. Referring to the panic which seized Nottingham in 1991, he warned that these nasty rumours, acting upon young minds, could well be a cause of actual satanic manifestations in times to come.

28

Just a Coincidence

December 1993

*A*n American woman I know told me of something strange that happened when she was a little girl. It was a few years after the War and she was sitting with her father in the local soda bar enjoying an ice cream. A man came in, and the father recognised him as an old comrade whom he had not seen and barely thought of since they were in the Army together. He rose to greet him but then realised that it was the wrong man and sat down disappointed. A few minutes later another man came through the door and he indeed was the father's old Army friend.

I once kept a Coincidence Diary, noting down all the things of that kind which happened day by day; and I found, as others had done before, that the more I noticed them the more frequently they occurred. If I thought about someone he would immediately call or write; words I had previously never heard of repeated themselves in twos or threes; the clues in my crossword began giving personal messages; long-lost objects reappeared in places where they should always have been, and if I wanted a reference to any subject, I had only to pick up a book lying on someone's table and there it was. Life became so nervously intense that I grew tired of it, gave up the diary, and sank back into normality.

I think that during that period I was in a state of Primordial Perception, the state in which our primitive but highly sensitised nomadic ancestors lived. To live well, or at all, they had to be alert to all the clues and hints which nature provides, and know how to take advantage of them. They rode their luck not fatalistically but as they themselves made it, through the forms of sympathetic magic, which develop naturally from the primordial, spiritual mode of perception.

That is not a state in which one can comfortably live today. It clashes painfully with the modern way of perception, and those who discover or fall into it are liable to end up in the madhouse. Today one must muffle one's perceptions or the battery of signs and stimuli to which one is exposed would be overwhelming. We have our own special sensitivities, crossing the road without looking, for example, or understanding what a book is about just by scanning through it. It is quite a relief that we no longer have to worry much about ghosts, witches, hobgoblins, ominous birthmarks, or a strange shape that has appeared in a cloud. We can live pleasantly by modern reason and custom without having to rely upon luck and coincidences.

Yet the primordial perception is always at hand, and in times of shock or intense need it can take over, exposing its recipient to the underlying reality of our existence. Solzhenitzyn gives a good example in his description of a communist prison in Moscow. In the next-door cell was a famous physicist who was working out some formula or other and needed certain mathematical tables in order to continue. He did not exactly pray for these tables but he certainly very much desired them. His desire was answered that week when the library came round. They just gave you two books at random, usually items of party propaganda, and the physicist received one of these, together with the very book of mathematical tables he needed. Knowing this to be a miracle he quickly memorised the figures, and the next day an inspector came round, saw the book of tables, and angrily confiscated it.

I have just begun this important subject and it is time to stop. It will be continued, however, because the question of coincidences, how they occur and whether one can and should invoke them, seems to me to give the broadest possible hint at the nature of this world and how we fit into it.

29

Just Another Coincidence

January 1994

*L*ast time I wrote about the physicist in a Moscow prison, described by Solzhenitzyn, who so badly needed a certain technical book that he attracted it to himself from the communist gaol library.

I have had such experiences myself and have often read of other people's. In one of his many books, Colin Wilson says that while he was writing *The Occult,* he went to look up something in his extensive library and the book he needed fell off the shelf and opened at the right page.

My favourite was told by the popular science writer, Camille Flammarion. He was writing a chapter on the forces of the atmosphere when an atmospheric force entered his study and blew his pages out of the window into the street. A few days later he received proofs of the chapter from his publishers, complete with the missing sheets. The wind had deposited them in an orderly pile at the feet of a man who worked in the publisher's office, and he had picked them up assuming that he must have dropped them.

If you concentrate on something, particularly if you write about it, it tends to affect you personally. Writers on the occult, UFOs, global conspiracies, and so on often attract the phenomena of their subject, as unpleasant as they had imagined them. Strindberg's book *Inferno* tells much about what can happen in these circumstances. That is why I keep to the high ground.

In literary life coincidences are ever present. I once made a point of asking all the writers I knew if they had ever had such experiences, and all of them, not just the mystically inclined, had stories about being startled by some incident, which indicated a connection between their own minds and the world at large. Often they were similar to Solzhenitzyn's account, of books coming out of the blue at the moment they were needed, or of a library reference, which no amount of systematic research could have located, jumping out from a casually glanced-at page. Useful, indeed, but also rather shocking.

It would be pleasant to think that a benevolent world-spirit rewards honest searchers by fulfilling their prayers and desires, and sometimes it appears like that. But there are many coincidences which seem neither helpful nor meaningful and merely leave you gaping at the mystery.

The strangest one I heard was from the orator and playwright Heathcote Williams. About twenty years ago, while living in an attic room in Notting Hill, he felt inspired to write a play about the melancholy comedian Tony Hancock. As *Hancock's Last Half Hour*, it was a fine work and a great success, but Heathcote said he had no idea why he wrote it. The shock came while he was researching. He went to the BBC to see if they had any tapes of Hancock's old programmes; the only one available was of Hancock bemoaning his lot in a lonely bed-sit. To establish its seedy location the director had chosen a Notting Hill square, the very one that Heathcote was living in, and zoomed the camera up to a top-floor window, the actual window of Heathcote's room.

There is nothing better to do with this story than laugh at it, but I also take it, along with others such, as a kind of warning to accept the world as it is and as it comes rather than try vainly to explain anything, and not to interfere in the inscrutable. You can, I am sure, train your mind to make coincidences happen, concentrate your will and impose it to some extent on nature. The techniques are available from cults and business schools but I have no intention of studying them. Black magic can land you in deep water. You are better off accepting the rewards and punishments you are due in life, while adapting yourself to attract a preponderance of the former.

30
The Persistence of Crop Circles

October 1994

*T*he responsibilities I have incurred in taking on this column seem to me to be two-fold: first, to expose the errors in modern thought and conduct through the touchstone of constant truth and philosophy; and second, to keep you informed about things like crop circles.

Unreported by the press, this summer's display of designs imprinted on farmers' fields was magnificent. The formations were larger, finer, and more widespread than ever before. A consistent feature of this phenomenon is that it discredits every theory that purports to explain it. I had wondered how it was going to deal with the prevalent theory, that the whole thing is the work of unknown hoaxers, and I was deeply impressed by its response. Early in the season formations in oil-seed rape gave warning of exciting things to come, and my neighbour John Neal, owner of a scruffy canal boat, proposed a voyage down to Wiltshire to inspect the latest developments.

It took about a fortnight, navigating from Regent's Park up the Thames and into the cranky old Kennet and Avon canal at Reading. On the way we called at the riverside mansion of Uri Geller, recently vilified in *The Oldie*. We found there a handsome, charming Israeli gent, as honestly confused as the rest of us, who willingly demonstrated those "gifts of the Spirit" with which, through no fault or virtue of his own, he has been endowed.

After many days on the canal we finally moored up at the Barge Inn near Alton Barnes in the heart of crop-circle country. That, it turned out, was the pub chosen by the "croppies" for their evening gatherings and blatherings. The leading experts—American, German, and British—showed their faces there; news and rumours were at their hottest; ufologists, skeptics, philosophers, and cunning rustics mingled together and the conversation was the best in Wiltshire. Midsummer evenings outside the Barge Inn, with good fare and good company, and with the four elements—earth, air, fire, water—were exactly as you can remember them in the Golden Age.

The crop formations we saw were fantastic. Approaching Devizes on the main road from the north you were confronted by a field-long scorpion and, if you stopped, you could read scrawled notices by the maddened farmer denouncing it as mindless vandalism. As perceived, it was a work of art, and so were many of the other designs in wheat fields around Avebury and the old Wessex sanctuaries. Circles often appeared in the same fields as in previous years, infuriating landowners who suspected they were being mocked by their peasantry. From Devon and Sussex to Yorkshire and the North, crop circles this year were spotted all over England.

The designs are intelligent, so (unless you want to think the unthinkable) they must surely be man-made. One thing I learnt from my week at the Barge Inn is that certain people have become obsessed and are inspired by dreams or inner compulsions to imitate the original patterns or to surpass them in artistry. The phenomenon has taken to using human agents to further its work. That work has to do with the changing of minds. I do not say this lightly but because I have observed the effects of crop circles on the minds of those who have fallen under their spell. In some cases the result has been personal shipwreck—which was no doubt deserved and needed—but others have been awakened to an interest in life generally. These are times of revelation and crop circles are a powerful catalyst in this process. That is not a theory or opinion, just straightforward perception.

*What has happened
to time? Why is there now so little of it
compared to the amount there used to be?*

31

Dreams of Ape-Men

June 1993

The most learned creatures who have ever, as the evolutionists like to put it, "roamed the earth" are undoubtedly the Germans. I was impressed, therefore, to read in the papers that scientists of the Friedrich Schiller University at Jena have finally discovered something that evolutionists have always been looking for, a relic of an "ape-man." What they actually found was a small sliver of skull-bone.

To those who can read such things this bone tells a long, detailed story. Its owner, say the savants of Jena, was "human ape, just over five feet tall, with a life expectancy of twenty-eight years. He had a low, ape-like forehead and hair covered his body. His favourite dish was a type of wild rhinoceros that roamed the forest." Like his German descendants today, "he had developed powers of deduction, and he even had a good memory."

It is amazing how they can tell these things. Sherlock Holmes was given powers of deduction which exceeded those of any real individual. He could tell you all sorts of personal details about yourself just by looking at you, but even he needed an actual, living person to go by rather than just a bit of bone.

The evolutionists of Jena have long been famous for their ape-men. The founder of their cult was Ernst Haeckel, a contemporary of Charles

91

Darwin, who conceived the notion that humanity was descended from an arboreal ape by way of an intermediary species, which he named Pithecanthropus (Ape-Man). Since there was no evidence of any such creature he could imagine it as he liked, and he chose to depict it as a fat, slug-like monster covered with hair. A German artist, von Marx, anticipated the nightmare imagery of Francis Bacon in his portrait of Pithecanthropus with wife and baby, and this ogrish family became the centrepiece of the Haeckel Museum in Jena.

Despite what they say in Jena, no physical trace of any ape-man has effectively come to life and is now an active participant in human affairs. From out of Jena has come a *tulpa* or thought-form, a type of being who haunts the mind and sometimes emerges into the world of appearances. A few years after Haeckel designed his ape-man, creatures of similar aspect began to be observed in the Himalayas. Further sightings were reported from China and Asiatic Russia, and the United States became infested by a giant, hairy monster named Bigfoot because of the gigantic footprints it made in the snow. No one has ever caught or adequately photographed any of these creatures, nor is anyone likely to do so, for clearly they are not flesh-and-blood creatures but *tulpas*—psychic responses to the powerful collective dream of evolutionists everywhere, the dream of ape-men.

This may sound funny but actually it is quite unpleasant and dangerous. Below the surface of the human mind is a realm of ugly monsters, any one of which may, if allowed up into consciousness, become active in our experience of life. The giant, hairy ogre has his place in universal folklore, but as a supernatural monster, never as the ancestor of humanity. With their myth of human descent from this creature Haeckel and his colleagues gave it life and influence. Thus, unwittingly, they launched the colonial genocides of "primitive" nations and Hitler's extermination policy toward races he judged "subhuman." It is time now for the Jena people to stop their nonsense and turn from the manufacture of ape-men to investigating the wonders of the human mind, its powers of creating its own forms of reality, and the Universal Mind from which it proceeds.

What has happened to time? Why is there now so little of it compared to the amount there used to be?

32
Roll Your Own Superstitions

May 1998

Superstitions, like everything else, are subject to fashion. Merrily Harpur, the brilliant cartoonist who lives in Ireland, asked a neighbour if there was any local lore about swallows. Yes, he said, there is an old saying round here that they fly off and spend the winter in Africa. That notion is now widely accepted but, up until quite recently, respectable ornithologists would have scorned it, being persuaded by the evidence that swallows, swifts, martins, and other birds such as corn-crakes become torpid and hibernate in cracks and crevices. Linnaeus, Buffon, Cuvier, and their scientific peers were firm believers in torpid swallows, as were Gilbert White and most other notables up until the middle of the nineteenth century, when the Africa theory caught hold. This change of fashion brought total discredit to the old impeccably witnessed first-hand accounts of hibernating swallows discovered in holes and revived by warmth. For almost one hundred years no one questioned the new orthodoxy, but in the 1950s a professional American naturalist made scientific observations of whippoorwills hibernating in rock clefts and clusters of chimney swifts were found in hollow trees. Fashion changed again, and the last time I investigated this pet subject, the word was that even larger birds, such as ptarmigans and turkey vultures, sometimes go into hibernation. So much for the Irish folklore.

The truth, perhaps, is that some swallows—the ones you see on the telegraph wires discussing travel plans—fly off to Africa, while others prefer to hole up for the winter. If we were swallows I am sure that is how we would do it. That is a nice, easy-going sort of answer but it is not the popular sort. Popular demand is for cut-and-dried, one-or-the-other solutions, allowing you to feel enlightened by one opinion and to despise the other as superstition. Inevitably, in the course of time, one fashion gives way to another and we duly despise the orthodoxy that preceded ours. It is a stupid process but an interesting one, and I am enjoying a good laugh at an example of it just seen in *The Daily Telegraph*. Melinda Wittstock's article says that a new superstition has arisen among the decorators and property dealers of New York. The old fad, you will remember, was feng shui. The new one is called smudging. I have come across this smudging with American tour groups at Cornish stone circles. They light a bunch of sage and waft the smoke over you. Apparently the Red Indians do it, and in the full-blown New York property version it is not just sage but drums, rattles, chanting, and coloured lights that constitute proper smudging. Its purpose is to drive out evil spirits and attract lucky ones, and there are impressive testimonials to how well it works. Immediately after a good smudging, apartments long languishing on the market are sold for more than the asking price, and people become happy in rooms where they had previously felt uneasy.

It sounds a harmless practice and if it really works then we should all take it up. But I feel that by the time you or I get round to smudging, fashion will have moved on, taking away its magic. After you have earned a free bus pass you are no longer agile enough to chase fashion. What we need is the secret behind all forms of superstition, the secret of attracting good luck. The essential first step to that, I suggest, is to get rid of fixed opinions on all subjects, from the swallow question to the existence and nature of God, and to perceive the reality of our dependence on the world of spirit. You are then free to make your own coincidences. As a smoker and a free bus rider, I have found a way of making the bus come. I just begin rolling a cigarette. So far it has worked every time.

33
Demonic Reality

March 1997

*I*t is remarkable how few people today are prepared to talk about demons. There is willing belief in angels and my American friends often tell me about UFO crashes, alien abductions, and the infiltration of governments by malevolent space brothers. But if you inform them that most UFO phenomena are demonic or phantomesque, they have no idea what you are talking about. That is typical of the "modern mind" that I keep complaining about. Having cast off the traditional myths and expressions, the modern mind is receptive to notions of any kind, however stupid or degraded. That is one form of demonic possession.

It is not that I truly believe in demons, or in anything else for that matter, but you cannot deny Confucius, and he said that it is best to act as though such things existed. That is also what Patrick Harpur says in his book *Daimonic Reality,* about recurrent types of unexplained phenomena. Its title refers to those *daimones,* named by the ancient Greeks as the causes of both good and bad luck and all kinds of weird happenings. Harpur suggests that this concept of a daimonic realm is the most effective way of coming to terms with the strangeness of our existence. You could call him a fairyland revivalist, but that would imply sentimentalism, and Harpur's stand for the traditional, aesthetic language of demonology against the space-fantasies created by the modern mind is impeccably reasoned. His account of the daimonic realm, its questionable attributes, and its uncertain influence upon our lives strikes me as more relevant to actual human experience than any modern work of science or psychology.

But then I wonder, do we really want demons back again, and all the spook paraphernalia that goes with them? In the old tales, Robin Goodfellow with his train of imps and elves was remembered with affection as merry though mischievous, but many people must have found him intolerable, for a great deal of effort was spent in exterminating him and his kind. The early Christians were engaged in perpetual war against demons, praying, chanting, and ringing bells to expel them from their haunts. Church bells were invented as a powerful weapon for blasting away the local gods of paganism. An amusing poem of Chaucer described the riff-raff preachers who infested the countryside and exorcised spirits in every house and corner. Women, he says, are now free from molestation by elves, but the old incubi have been replaced by the preachers themselves. It all came to the same thing, no doubt, but it is easy to see why respectable women of the Middle Ages might have preferred a young friar to some ancient rustic demon.

Yet, on the whole, I think Patrick Harpur is right and that demonology remains an essential part of the human syllabus. In no other terms is it possible to comprehend, for example, the recurrent, long-recorded phenomenon of animal mutilation, a demonic plague that is still very active in the western United States. How else can you sensibly regard yetis and Loch Ness monsters than as phantom products of another reality? Why bring in extra-terrestrials when every book of folklore tells you that elves and fairies are behind the abduction experience? It is not spacemen but the gods of good luck that sometimes lead me to the very book and page I need in the London Library. These creatures are everywhere because they occur naturally in our minds. If you do not call them demons you call them "germs" or "toxins," eat health foods and worry yourself to death on their account. You might as well recognise that the world is basically spiritual and adopt the appropriate terminology.

34

The Demons among Us

November 2000

*J*ust as I was crossing the street, with one step to go, the lights went green and a monstrous great jeep-like thing lurched forward at me, causing me to skip hurriedly onto the pavement. I spun round to scream or spit at the driver, but too late. He was already bellowing through his window and in the second before he sped away I glimpsed a huge, circular red face, fringed with hair and with a noisy black hole gaping at its centre. It reminded me of Plato's account of the afterlife in *The Republic,* where a "bellowing mouth" hurls back into hell those who try to escape from it. The sight of it was so amazing that I began laughing, and a youth standing beside me who had seen the incident, laughed too, so it was a happy moment. But I felt sorry for the miserable thug in his bullying car because I could see clearly that he was in the grip of a nasty, low-grade sort of demon. From what I observe and hear from others, a fair number of motorists are possessed by it.

Psychologists and believers in Science do not care for this sort of talk. Demonic possession, they say, is an ignorant, out-of-date explanation for the various types of mental illness which doctors can now treat and sometimes cure. That is one way of looking at it, but I have known people who could most simply and naturally be called possessed. On one occasion an American visitor, who had come to talk to me about his

UFO experiences, was suddenly convulsed and a different voice spoke through him. It was a powerful demon, uttering certain home truths together with threats, the gist of them being that it had sent the man to kill me. He, brave soul, was struggling against it and in a moment of self-control he urged me to run away, which I was glad to do. Later, I heard, the devil prevailed and he killed someone. Paranoid schizophrenia, they said.

When you have cleared your mind of psychologists' claptrap and can see things through your own eyes and reason, you begin to realise how densely we are now infested with demonic forces. It is not just individuals that are possessed by them, but official institutions of state of culture. The media is dominated by their filthy propaganda, so is the world of fashion, and in the arts they openly flaunt themselves. Sluts, creeps, and gay gangsters award each other grants and prizes for works whose only content is scandal, while Beelzebub, spirit of confusion and Lord of the Philistines, presides over the rubbish in his Tate Modern temple on the Thames. If, as seems likely, the reign of the Antichrist is now upon us, it is to the credit of the art people that they are plainly exhibiting it.

The modern mind has no room for demons and ascribes them to the Dark Ages. That is unfair, because the ages in which spiritual reality was commonly recognised were not always dark but included every great period of civilisation—and indeed every period except our own. The reasoning of learned men down the ages is that we live in a divine creation and are guided by powers that transcend the human will. That accords with the new findings in physics, and I can add other reasons for accepting it as the best possible view of things. It stops me from worrying about the Antichrist, demons at the Tate, or the bellowing mouth that drove its car at me. These are the due manifestations of our time, the entertainments that are now provided, and we might as well enjoy them—just as the citizens of Babylon enjoyed the last days of their mighty city before the weeping began. It is obvious that everything today is going downhill, or to hell, but that is not our concern. We just happen to be on stage at this moment. And there are other scenes yet to come.

35

Lost and Found

May 2000

*A*ll over the world, people know of some god or demon who can be called upon to find mislaid objects. St. Anthony does it for Catholics and in Morocco there is Sidi Hadji or some such name, famous among hippies for finding lost bits of dope. There has been correspondence about this recently in *Fortean Times* magazine, beginning with a letter about a lost bunch of keys. The writer's sister knew where she had put them down, but they had disappeared and were nowhere to be found. He persuaded her to join him in asking aloud for their return and then they sat for about ten minutes in silence. She looked toward the pile of papers where she remembered leaving them but the keys were not there. Seconds later she looked again and there they were!

This letter brought forth other instances of the same miraculous effect. A common observation was of things vanishing from their usual place and returning some time later of their own accord, without invocation. One writer who had worked in a television library said that the usual practice in his department, whenever a tape or film went missing, was to wait a while and then look again in the same place. Among librarians, he said, this is well known for being effective. An example he gave was of a missing tape found "teetering on the edge of its shelf" as if begging to be found. Colin Wilson has a similar story, of a book he was looking for that seemed to throw itself off its shelf, falling open at the page he needed.

In explanation for this another *Fortean Times* reader pointed to quantum theory, according to which an object can be in two places at once, move into another time or dimension and reappear when someone looks for it. Keys are frequent performers of this lost-and-found trick and so are rings and books. Many stories, some mythical, others apparently genuine, tell of a precious ring lost overboard and rediscovered by the owner within a fish served up for dinner.

As for books, the anecdotes are endless. Many years ago I became aware of the "library-angel" effect, asked other writers about it, and heard some near-incredible accounts of desired books and references turning up out of the blue.

Also heard of, and personally experienced, were incidents of the book that left its place, was searched for in vain, and was later found just where it always should have been.

Being of somewhat Low Church persuasion, I do not call upon saints or demons but take these blessings as they come, and I am grateful to the process. And I am encouraged in this attitude by *Fortean Times* letter-writer Pearl Oliver of Crewe, who revealed the dangerous secret of how to get anything you want in this world. The one to ask is Satan, the owner of all material things.

She tried it at a bus stop by a lonely road on a cold winter's afternoon. "Satan, send me a bus!" Immediately two buses came. She tried it again and once more Satan responded, so instantly and precisely that she was "shocked enough never to do it again, as the returns seemed a trifle paltry in payment for my immortal soul." Her last experience was with a Catholic friend. She had incautiously told him about Satan's power and he insisted upon trying it. Laughingly he asked for a condom, and soon afterward he went out into the street where he tripped over something. It was a bag stuffed with condoms. He screamed with terror and for the rest of the evening did nothing but mumble Hail Marys.

People do sell their souls. You read about them in newspapers and it is easy enough to envy their wealth and renown. But these, as Pearl Oliver reminds us, are paltry at the price and they do not last. There are ways of attracting luck, innocently, harmlessly, and to everyone's benefit, but that is something we shall have to go into another time.

What has happened
to time? Why is there now so little of it
compared to the amount there used to be?
...properly into those

36
The Flight from Reason

November 1993

$\mathcal{T}$he only newspaper which conveys any idea of what is going on is *The Telegraph*. In mid-October, for example, it reported that the Indian government has mobilised its snake-charmers, sending them round schools and factories to give lectures on the menace of AIDS. People were more inclined to listen to them than to the health officials. In the next column was news from Malaysia about the health programme and how it is largely conducted by the traditional witch-doctors, who also control business and politics. The dismembered corpse of a well-known politician had just been found, ritually murdered by these magical mobsters. Then there was a story about a holy icon that had been snatched from a state museum and used for magical purposes by one of the sides in the recent civil strife in Moscow. In Greece the head of the Orthodox Church was calling upon the drought-stricken nation to join in religious practices for rain-making; Muslim enthusiasts were killing Russians in Algeria; Aborigines were demanding the return of their old ritual centres . . . and that was in just one day's "Foreign News" section.

As *Telegraph* readers must know by now, foreigners are strange people, prone to irrationalities; but they are in the majority, and we ought to pay some attention to what they are doing and thinking on the far side of the Channel. The signs are ominous. It looks as if they have finally seen through us, as they were bound to do one day. The British cannot rule forever and personally I am glad to see the end of it. Our innovations have brought enough plagues upon the world. It began, said William Blake, with priestcraft, first invented by our ancient Druids who spread it to the Jews and others. That I can well believe. We have always been known for our obstinacy in making other countries accept whatever fad or notion is prevailing among us. Innumerable thought-forms—industrialism, imperialism, Protestantism, Puritanism, Darwinism, socialism—have issued from these islands to spread confusion among foreigners, not to mention those playful causes of international rancor: cricket, tennis, and football. Most effective of all the influences we have let loose is the spirit of Modernism, the ruination of traditional standards everywhere. In brewing up that spirit we were, of course, greatly helped by the rationalistic French, the idealistic Germans, and our other European neighbours.

The world is now turning against us and the old atavisms, as we once called them—tribalism, animism, nationalistic religion—are reasserting their reality. It had to happen, and it is futile to regret the inevitable victory of Eternity over Modernism, of the witch-doctor over the man with the stethoscope, the snake-charmer over the savant, the charismatic over the country vicar. It is all prophesied and now it can be seen actually happening, the Beast ascending from the abyss for his allotted period of reign.

Nothing in this world lasts forever. One day, in accordance with the cycle, reason will be restored, but never again will arise that spurious form of reason, identified with Modernism and largely British-made, which urges us to lay waste the earth and our own cultures. Good riddance to that, but I am afraid we shall have cause to miss it; for it is all part of that great South Sea Bubble, which includes the present worldwide economics set-up; and when it bursts we shall look pretty foolish, being wholly dependent upon it and quite unable to manage by ourselves. We should never have interfered in the first place.

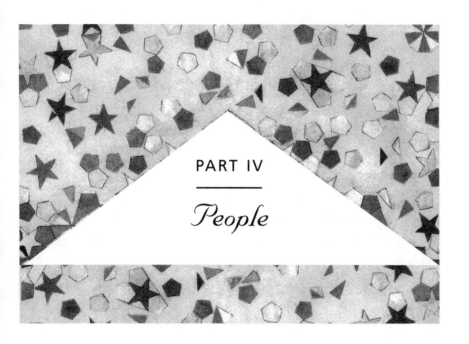

PART IV

People

37
Beyond the New Age

September 1998

*A*t the risk of sounding like your old schoolmaster, who said this about what?

"It is coeval with the universe itself; and however its continuity may be broken by opposing systems, it will make its appearance at different periods of time, as long as the sun himself shall continue to illuminate the world."

The same person also said on the same subject: "It is the greatest good in which man can participate: for it purifies us from the defilements of our passions and assimilates us to Divinity, it confers upon us the proper felicity of our nature."

These things were said about 200 years ago by Thomas Taylor, and he was talking about the philosophy, science, and esoteric doctrines of Plato, which is what he always talked about.

The code of knowledge and the way of seeing, thinking, and living associated with Plato were not Thomas's own invention but came to him along that "golden chain" of initiated teachers and mystagogues, beginning in deepest antiquity, passing through Egypt and Ancient Greece into the Western world and carried on by certain scholars, poets, and revivalists into the present. That is how Thomas

Taylor saw it, and so did William Blake and W. B. Yeats, and so does Kathleen Raine, and, since the best story is likely to be the truest, I enjoy believing it too.

In the reliable newspaper I read it says that 40 million Americans partake in the self-realisation movement—from therapy victims to cultists, New Agers, and UFO abductees. That means about 40 million deluded souls, captivated by *daimons* and illusory thought-forms. There is an infinite number of these, but truth is one and the same. The way to it is not widely advertised; you never see Plato in a New Age bookshop. But Thomas Taylor insisted that only through Platonic studies and practices can true knowledge be drawn out from our prenatal memories and established in the rational mind. Anyone who discovers and persists in these studies, he promised, and achieves the state of wisdom to which they lead, sanctifies himself and all round him, gaining peace of mind, a life of grace, and a divinely blessed soul.

For the enlightenment of English-speaking humanity, Taylor spent a long lifetime translating Plato, Aristotle, the Neo-Platonists, and others in the golden chain, adding copious notes and commentaries in explanation of the philosophic mysteries.

If it really is true, as Plato reasoned and Taylor proclaimed, that wisdom and happiness are to be found in the study of true philosophy, you would expect the whole self-realisation movement to plunge into Plato, as edited by Thomas Taylor. There is of course a catch; philosophy gives nothing to dabblers and dilettanti but demands total dedication. "Most people," said Taylor, "are so ignorant that they do not even know that there is anything worth knowing. The best thing they can do is carry on with their 'sordid avocations' until they receive due punishment and are purged."

If you want to pursue the "greatest good" you can easily do so now, thanks to a new forged link in the golden chain—Tim Addey of the Prometheus Trust, 17 Rossiters Hill, Frome, Somerset. He is in the middle of publishing the whole of Taylor's translation work in thirty-four volumes, as a means of reforming education. Or you can subscribe to Kathleen Raine's *Temenos* magazine. Or you can muddle along with your sordid avocation, which cannot be such a bad option, since Plato assured us that "things are better taken care of than can possibly be imagined."

38

A Man You Can Trust

January 1994

*H*aving sifted out the moralisers, systematisers, and word-quibblers, I am left with two philosophers as guiding beacons and masters of soothsaying. One is old Plato, the purveyor of the universal tradition to the West, and the other is Charles Fort (1874–1932) of the Bronx. Both were great poets and mythmakers, though equally scornful of poetic vanities, and their views of the nature of the world, existence, and reality were essentially the same though arrived at from different directions. Neither of them recommended any system of belief. Rather, they extended their art to expressing as finely as possible the truth about our human situation, and they both made use of fabulous tales to illustrate how things really are.

Every year the merry Forteans of America celebrate the all-accommodating worldview of Charles Fort at a gathering in the federal capital, Washington D.C. Lectures are given by backwoodsmen with theories, Bigfoot-hunters, UFO-abductees, and revolutionary interpreters of ancient hieroglyphics. You feel that anything could happen there but actually it is always the same; you drink a lot of weak beer with the most interesting, original, independent, or crackpot thinkers that the country harbours, and return home cheerfully encouraged.

If, as I suspect, Fort's philosophy can make you happier and more at ease in the world than any other—while avoiding artificiality and wishful thinking—then it is my duty to spread it around. Like Plato he saw the universe as a self-regulating organism influenced by nothing outside because outside it there is nothing. Nor is there really anything inside it, because everything else is just a part of it, influenced by outside forces and without any real individuality. "Nothing can ever be proved," said Fort, "because there is no Thing there to be proved. The only existing example of any actual, independent entity, the only manifestation of Number One as the philosophers put it, is the universe itself. Nothing else is fully real, our own existence being intermediate between reality and unreality, order and chaos, the positive and the negative."

Yet we all aspire to reality. Every thing, creature, nation, notion, theory, soul, and person tries to make itself more real than all the rest. "Our whole existence," said Fort, "is a striving for the positive state." Systems of religion and science pretend to reality by ignoring for as long as possible the data that contradict them. Fort collected those data. He did not regard them as facts, seeing that in an indeterminate world there could be no such thing, but his records of unexplained happenings were impeccably derived from scientific books and journals. The data he selected could no more and no less be called fact than those that support every established theory and worldview.

Fort used his data to create many alternative world-pictures, looking always for the most "inclusive" expressions, encompassing the fullest possible range of human experience and thus approaching most nearly to the status of reality. Plato's all-inclusive universe was similar except that he made it the work of a Creator. Fort's comment was that he had never heard of a creator that was not itself created, and he got round the problem by saying that the universe is our reality and there is no need for metaphysics. That tells you why Fortean philosophers are so comparatively happy. They expect nothing from this world but what it happens to give, nor do they feel impelled to prove or justify anything, seeing that we are all part of the universal creature, which in its own cranky, idiosyncratic way more or less looks after its own.

What has happened to time? Why is there now so little of it compared to the amount there used to be?

39

The Philosopher's Ideal Woman

February 1994

They say that I have been writing too much about cosmology lately, and that many readers of this journal are ladies who do not care for that sort of thing. I had thought, actually, that I was writing mostly for ladies. It seems to me that women are more susceptible to philosophy, as opposed to quibbling and showing off, than men generally are. That must be why old Epicurus accepted only young girls as his pupils and taught them in his garden.

The type of person I imagine myself to be in communication with in this column is the wise, witty spinster who appears in novels by that most orthodox epicurean writer, Thomas Love Peacock. He was a devotee of St. Catherine of Alexandria, patron saint of virgins, weavers, philosophers, and the pure in heart, and with her in mind he created his most attractive female characters. In *Gryll Grange* her legend is related by young Mr. Falconer, who lives in a forest tower dedicated to St. Catherine, and is waited upon by seven lovely sisters, whose virginal chorus beguiles his winter evenings.

St. Catherine was a type of Sophia or Athena, goddess of wisdom. Inspired by Christ, she argued down the fifty learned philosophers whom the Roman emperor sent against her. These he put to death together with his empress and leading general whom the saint had also converted. St. Catherine's sentence was to be torn to pieces on a spiked wheel, but divine intervention broke the device, and she was finally beheaded. Angels carried her body to a peak of Mount Sinai and from there it was conveyed down to a monastery, which has ever since been a resort of pilgrims.

In the Middle Ages (through, it is said, the mysterious machinations of the Knights Templar) the cult of St. Catherine became highly popular in Western Europe. The Sorbonne and other centres of learning adopted her as their patron and in folk custom she became the benefactor of young women, particularly in affairs of love and marriage. On her feast day, 25 November, women in need of husbands, or a change of husbands, visited her shrines and invoked her aid.

If you want to marry or remarry, or if you are just an old antiquarian with a love for secluded sanctuaries, you will certainly be rewarded by visits to St. Catherine's ancient chapels, many of them near the south coast of England. Typically they are on green, rounded hilltops, in feminine contrast to the spikier St. Michael sites, with a holy well at their foot and often upon an ancient pilgrim's route. A fine example is the ruined chapel at Guildford, where the Pilgrim's Way crosses the River Wey on its eastward course from another St. Catherine's hill, above Winchester. Peacock, who lived on the Wey, knew the spot well and tells of a mystical connection between St. Catherine's at Guildford and two sisterly hill chapels nearby, those of St. Martha and St. Anne.

South Dorset is the richest country for St. Catherine's followers. Her chapel at Milton Abbas, approached by a flight of steps cut into a hill above the abbey, was a well-known place of magic for procuring husbands, as also was the queen of all our St. Catherine sites, the remarkable stone chapel above Abbotsbury. Overlooking the sea, and once providing a beacon for mariners, it is on top of a steep hill, the sides of which are scored with ridges forming the pattern of a giant labyrinth, symbol of the Mysteries. A similar lighthouse-chapel was at St. Catherine's Point, the southernmost tip of the Isle of Wight. At these and other St. Catherine sites one learns to appreciate the old religious artistry, which expressed the character of a wise, kind, beautiful virgin martyr in terms of natural adapted features in a sanctified landscape.

40

Our Silent Queen

August 1998

*I*t was very rude of Mr. Paisley to call the Queen a parrot. He meant that she never speaks for herself but simply repeats parrot-like everything that her Prime Minister tells her. It was rude but it hit the nail on the head. In the course of her long reign Elizabeth has seen more radical changes in the kingdom than any previous monarch. Yet no audible squawk, no personal word of encouragement, warning, or condemnation, has come out of her. I am told she is painfully shy and that she was brought up in a defeatist atmosphere by educators who thought the communists would take over and that she would do best to keep quiet. Certainly she must keep out of politics, but not all our national affairs are political. The way we behave at football matches, for example; that has nothing to do with the government. It was quite inappropriate for Mr. Blair to criticise the conduct of our World Cup supporters, to apologise for them to the French and call upon their employers to sack them on their return home. We elected his party to administer the state, not to teach us manners. Only the Queen is in a position to do that. But she, of course, said nothing to the hoolies and allowed the Minister to usurp her function.

At her coronation in the Abbey, Elizabeth was seated upon the

Stone of Jacob, the crown of St. Edward with its twelve jewels (symbolising the twelve tribes of types of humanity) was placed on her head and she was anointed as a high priest of Israel (God's people). By these and other solemn acts she was dedicated to the service of God and to maintaining the religious, constitutional, and popular rights of her subjects. Her reward for this was a life of luxury and the satisfaction of all her needs and wants. It can hardly be said that she has kept her side of the bargain.

On the insistence of her Ministers, with no demand from her people and no form of explanation to them, she has consented to changes which at the beginning of her reign would barely have been thinkable. Metrication, for example; she could easily, harmlessly, with popular approval, and in accordance with her oath have rejected the atheistic metre and upheld true standards. Then she was told to yield up her own sovereignty and her people's self-government to a cabal of unknown Eurocrats. Finally, on the whim of a Prime Minister, she permitted the stone on which she was crowned, a source and symbol of her authority, to be wrenched from its chair in the Abbey and carried out of England. There are prophecies connected with that and they are not favourable to the survival of England's monarchy. I would not care to call Elizabeth a parrot; it is more like a case of sleep-walking.

A queen who says nothing and does nothing on behalf of traditional liberties or even her own prerogatives—is the King Log type of monarch worth having? It is hard for a born-and-bred monarchist to answer No to that question, but I do so for patriotic reasons. A queen who does anything the government tells her is a danger to the country because the government can then do anything in her name and there is no appeal. Perhaps we should follow the old Scandinavians, who replaced their king with a respectable, elderly scholar, appointed by the twelve members of the high council who represented the sovereign crown. He knew by heart the law of his people and acted as a one-man court of appeal. I can think of several people who would be excellent in that position, who would be completely honourable and know how to keep the government in order. Yehudi Menuhin would be my choice, or Lord Longford, or Roderick O'Connor (a potential High King of Ireland) or honest Ken Livingstone. If you want a woman, what about Lady Thatcher who has always coveted the queenly role? And what about the noble-minded Prince Charles?

41
Building the Future

March 1996

*I*f you hear of something good you do not always want to shout about it for fear of cheapening it. Writing in *The Oldie,* however, I feel less inhibited, because the level of civilised discourse maintained in this journal allows me to speak seriously with little danger of being taken too literally. One of the good things about living in England is that it is difficult to become self-important and didactic here; one has plenty of old friends to remind one of how insignificant one really is. These remarks introduce my panegyric on the Prince of Wales's Institute of Architecture.

The Patron of this Institute is well known for his weaknesses, but I am not interested in his problems with women, having had enough of my own. A philosopher is not *homo genitalis;* his record is exemplified by Plato, who abjured sexual activity, and Socrates, who married a bitch (or made a good woman into one).

Prince Charles's strength is that he is an idealist, possibly the world champion of his kind. He once said that he would like to "stop corruption throughout the world." We lesser idealists gasp at that, but we cannot help admiring its princely breadth of vision; as our man Plato said, one must first imagine the absolute ideal and then be prepared to compromise. The Institute of Architecture reflects this pragmatic idealism.

If you think the world can be changed through art and architecture and you found an Institute to implement those changes, the best thing you can do is involve Keith Critchlow in it. He is a practicing architect and the best-informed, most effective teacher of the Pythagorean science—the science of number, harmony, and proportion. He represents a tradition which has inspired architecture in all its greatest periods, together with the societies in which it has flourished. One of the best things that has happened in our times is that Prince Charles met Keith Critchlow and had the discernment to establish his influence at the centre of his school of architecture and the traditional arts.

Discernment is the ultimate product of the Pythagorean science. Throughout daily life one is faced with numerous decisions, and if one is well balanced and at ease, one is more likely to make the appropriate choices. The same is true in architecture and the arts generally.

We have seen in our lives a great many monstrous creations by megalomaniacs, egomaniacs, and technolaters, the creations of uneasy, uncentred minds. It was not the fault of our brilliant architects that they built in such arrogant, inhuman style; it was because their minds were chaotic and untrained.

The noble, revolutionary purpose of the Prince of Wale's Institute is to remedy that complaint by equipping its students with the ability to discern what is ugly, pretentious, and disproportionate, while centring their minds on the eternal sources of beauty and truth. That is easier said than done, but there is a certain way toward it, a certain course of study, which infallibly benefits the mind and establishes a sense of justice and proportion within it. Those studies are almost nowhere available except at the Institute under the direction of Critchlow and his colleagues.

A huge weight of academic disapproval bears down upon the Institute. The atheists dislike it; the technophiles despise it; its royal Patron's pathetic desire for popular approval stirs up the bullies of the press against it. It is unfashionable and very far from perfect, but it is rare and valuable for being on the right course. Maybe it will change the world a bit, and for the better.

42

Enoch Powell
and the West Indians

March 1998

*E*noch Powell has died and I am sorry to hear it. He was a man of high principles and perception, grounded in classical, orthodox scholarship. As a world leader he would have stood out among the confused tyrants and toadies who set the tone of modern politics. Alas, it was not to be. Like any honest philosopher, Powell was at a disadvantage in competing for the popular vote. Most of us want to continue as we are rather than face inconvenient realities. That is why we elect the sort of people that Plato called "panders." They cater for our whims rather than our interests. Who has the ear of Downing Street? It is not that enlightened jewel of our nation, Yehudi Menuhin, but the loutish Gallagher brothers.

About thirty years ago Powell raised the question of coloured immigration, especially the mass influx of West Indians. He prophesied trouble to come and advocated repatriation. This struck a chord among the working classes, who bore the brunt of immigration, but it ended Powell's career as a serious politician. Our liberal friends, who would never consider letting their spare flat to a poor black family, denounced him as a "racialist," thus sidestepping his arguments. One of the few who spoke up in Enoch's favour was the Trinidadian militant, Michael X (Michael de Freitas to us civilians). His objection to the multi-cultural racial experiment was that sweet-natured, God-fearing West Indian children were being corrupted and deculturised by the English education system—undisciplined, atheistic, and shot through with Darwinian assumptions of the white man's natural supremacy. Investigating the English mentality, Michael came across Darwin's *Descent of Man* and read in it that black people are just a cut above the ape and doomed to extinction, giving way to the civilised Europeans.

Not being a Darwinian, I do not believe in the hierarchy of species or that one kind of man is more developed than another. At the same time we are all obviously different. Chess grandmasters are likely to be Russian Jews, the ping-pong champion is an Oriental, whilst sprinting and boxing events are dominated by African types. The explanation, according to us religious people, is that God wants to be praised through a symphony of many voices rather than a monotonous chorus. Equally religious is my way of avoiding Powell's question of whether or not a mixed-race society is a practical proposition. Since it has happened here, it must have been God's will.

Having lived through the immigration period, I have the impression that it has gone remarkably smoothly. We do not need so many black misfits, but West Indians generally seem like an old-fashioned version of ourselves—keen sportsmen, humorous talkers, beer-drinking cricket lovers, with simple Protestant inclinations. They fill churches and chapels abandoned by the English and praise the Lord in no uncertain manner. Unfortunately they hardly ever seem to go to the country or seaside, so they know far too little about their new islands. I feel, as Mr. Powell probably did, that the modern, multi-racial armed forces lack something of the blind, do-or-die patriotism that inspired young men in the old days. But is this entirely a bad thing? So many heroes on both sides were sacrificed in the First World War that the slaughter was prolonged beyond sense. I do not think the men would stand for it today, nor should they. An old friend from

Granada said to me, "You English should be thankful to have us West Indians among you." At the time I was so taken aback that I forgot to ask what exactly he meant, but I have thought about it a great deal since and have found good reasons for thinking that he may have been right.

43

Science for Us Simple Folk

April 1995

*E*ver since 1981 when he entered print with *A New Science of Life,* I have been a keen reader of Rupert Sheldrake's books. He is a scientist of an unusual kind. Like Richard Milton, whose books have been acclaimed in *The Oldie,* he is neither an atheist nor an ignoramus but ideally qualified to bust the racket of modern science. You can tell how well he is doing by the reaction from that shaky establishment. His first book was greeted by Maddox, editor of *Nature,* with a call for it to be burned! Against the emotional opposition Sheldrake remains calm and polite, returning sweet reason to intemperate abuse.

His latest book, *Seven Experiments That Could Change the World,* is recommended to everyone who has enjoyed this column. It tells you far more about the nature of the world than Hawking's unreadable best seller. It is written so simply that you or I can understand and feel personally engaged in the subject. If it does change the world, it will be in our direction, toward an acknowledged reality based on our own senses and experience of life rather than on the dicta of academic obscurantists. This is the only worthwhile form of liberation. There is no need for rabid politics or shouting in the streets. The world will be changed and healed when we learn to respect our own perceptions of it.

Let us start simply, on common ground. All who act as companions for dogs or cats come to know that the animal is often aware of their intentions. Most commonly observed is the pet that knows when its owner is about to return home. Science pooh-poohs this phenomenon with smirks at the sentimentalists who recognise it. One way to change the world and wipe patronizing smiles off faces is to prove scientifically that we are right. We must have ourselves timed and recorded at the moment when we decide to return home. We must have someone else with a video on the dog, recording the moment when it begins its routine, running to the gate, jumping to the window or whatever. When the two coincide we . . . write to *The Field?* . . . inform the Royal Society? . . . badger the EC? No one seems responsible for supervising the change-over in worldviews, so the best we can do is write to Rupert Sheldrake, care of his publishers. He is one of those exemplary authors who (despite Oscar Wilde's advice) always acknowledges letters.

Can psychic pets change the world? Or Uri Geller? Not irresistibly, because Science does not abide by its own rules. It is not just a poor loser but a bare-faced cheat. Later in his book Sheldrake shows how it rigs the game; how scientists prove all kinds of nonsense by selective use of data; how the will of the experimenter determines the results he gets; how so-called constants and natural laws are merely conventional imaginings. Einstein's theory depended on the assumption that the speed of light is always the same. But it is not. Every experimenter has measured it differently. In 1972 Science passed a law defining the speed of light at a certain arbitrary figure and that now is what everyone has to go by.

As a man of science Sheldrake is not against his own profession but wants to reform it, to put it in touch with reality. Science without direction is a mind out of control, creating thought-forms with no regard for their social or aesthetic effects. It needs direction; and the only proper direction is toward the truth; and the only way toward truth is through that despised object that people kick in the gutter, that philosopher's stone, the old and reliable God-centred, simple, human way of seeing things.

44

Sheldrake and the Revolution

April 2000

*T*he *Oldie* readers' luncheons at Simpson's in the Strand are famous for good old-fashioned fare and company to match. So they are not to be missed. I was stupid enough to miss one last February simply because I forgot it. This forgetting business has become an embarrassment. Friends, engagements, even what I have just got up to do: all these pass out of memory and I am mortified. But to look on the bright side, a merciful veil has been drawn over past fiascos, and I cannot now be tempted by the vanity of writing memoirs.

The reason why I was so disappointed to have missed that *Oldie* luncheon was that Rupert Sheldrake spoke there. He too is not to be missed. The first time I met him was in 1981 at the Elephant Fayre, a genteel sort of pop festival which used to be held in Cornwall. That year there was a "debates tent" and Sheldrake and I were among speakers in a debate on evolution. His first book, *A New Science of Life,* had just come out and soon it was making headlines. That was because the editor of *Nature* and other bigwigs of science had denounced it. It was even said that the book should be publicly burnt. Shedrake's heresies were many but they all boiled down to religion. He rejected Darwin and materialists generally and spoke of "morphogenetic fields" which act like angels to create the various forms and patterns of nature.

124

And who created these fields? It must have been the Creator, said Sheldrake.

That made sense to me, but to science the name of God is like a red rag to a bull. Scientists assume atheism with their professional vows, and if one of their own kind mentions the dreaded name they feel betrayed. What infuriates them about Sheldrake is that he backs up his spiritual view of the world with strictly scientific experiments. One of these, described in his *Seven Experiments That Could Change the World,* is to prove that if you stare from behind at someone in a bus, the person becomes aware of it and turns round.

His new book, *Dogs That Know When Their Owners Are Coming Home,* says it all in the title. Most pet owners come to realise that their animals can read or anticipate their thoughts just as every "streetwise" lout knows about the staring effect. But Sheldrake's proofs of the obvious are not so much for simple people as for those whose superior scientific education has deprived them of normal human perceptions. His mission is to reform science, to abolish the conventions of materialism that still handicap it, and to turn it toward the reality of common spiritual experience. That would indeed change the world.

In this column two months ago I complained of being assailed by gloomy Darwinians, led by that demonically persuasive writer, Jared Diamond, and asked for readers' help. One reply was from Philip Blair, author of a new, hopeful book on the future. He said, "The problem with modern man is that he shies away from his manifestly spiritual dimension and seeks security in protesting an animal identity." That really hits the nail on the head. It explains the origin of our demoralised urban "underclass" and of that modern plague, "lack of self-esteem." If we believe we are just animals we will think and behave bestially, and if children cannot be told that we are all one people under God, where is our hope for the future? Materialistic science and the dreary, degrading Marxian view of things that goes with it have created a false picture of the world, and its effect on human happiness has been disastrous.

So I cherish dear Rupert Sheldrake, support his campaign, and admire the cool-headed, C-of-E, love-your-enemy spirit in which he conducts it. Times and thoughts are changing rapidly and I would not be surprised if he ended up as President of the Royal Society. In that event you will know that there really has been a revolution.

45

New Light on Old Stones

August 1996

*I*n the middle of a field crossed by a footpath I met someone walking the other way and said "Good morning." The man was highly embarrassed; his face twitched, he looked down at his boots and just managed to grunt as he went by. Call it shyness if you like, but deculturisation is my word for it. How different it is in Ireland. If music and conversation are what you go by, Irish popular culture is on a far higher level than our own, and by that standard the most cultured region in Western Europe is West Cork.

I was there recently, talking in pubs and visiting megalithic sites with the local expert in both departments, Jack Roberts. He is a pupil and former colleague of Martin Brennan, a meteoric character who appeared in Ireland about twenty years ago, blazed briefly through the world of Irish archaeology, and left it in a state of shock and scandal from which it has not recovered.

The most famous monuments of old Ireland are the great mound-temples, dating from the fourth millennium BC, with narrow, stone-lined passages leading to inner chambers. Poets ancient and modern have been attracted to these sites; mythological episodes are located there and they are rich in folklore. Archaeologists, however, regarded them as places of darkness where primitive, superstitious tribespeople interred their dead. With the coming of Martin Brennan they were transformed into temples of light. He began at Newgrange, one of the three great mounds which stand together with lesser monuments on the north bank of the River Boyne, not far from Dublin.

For fifty years the guide to its inner recesses, Mr. Hickey, had told visitors about the wonderful light beam which stole down the passage and illuminated the inner chamber at one moment of the year, midwinter sunrise. The authorities denied it and ridiculed the old man—until direct observations proved him right. Sad to say, the realisation came too late, for the mound had already been ruined. Tomb-theorists demolished and reconstructed its interior, and the trajectory of the light beam is no longer as it originally was. Encased in concrete and with an absurd pebbledash exterior, Newgrange is now a faked-up tourist attraction. Its giant neighbour, Knowth, is undergoing the same treatment; if you go there tomorrow you can observe its venerable fabric being torn apart by mechanical diggers.

With Jack and other enthusiasts Martin Brennan spent nights crouching within mound chambers all over Ireland and witnessed the light that penetrated into them on significant days of the lunar or solar calendar. In a cairn at Loughcrew I saw for myself how a thin ray from the equinoctial sunrise entered the chamber, lit upon the backstone and, as the sun climbed higher toward the south, moved correspondingly across the stone, picking out the symbols inscribed upon it. A message written more than 5,000 years ago was being spelt out before my eyes, but in a language totally unknown. If you ask what was the most exciting moment of my life: that was it.

As Brennan saw it, traditional Irish culture stems directly from the sacred science of the prehistoric mound builders. His discoveries, he believed, would spark off a revival. Suddenly and mysteriously he vanished from Ireland. His books—*The Boyne Valley Vision, The Stars and the Stones*—are no longer in print. The JCBs continue to plough through ancient mounds and you could easily conclude that Brennan's renaissance fizzled out.

Yet, as we Druids say, truth will prevail. In numbers and influence the Brennanites are growing ever stronger. When you are next in West Cork you can easily find Jack Roberts's megalithic guidebooks, finely illustrated by his own pen, and if you track him down and invite him for a drink you may hear the whole story. You may then experience the mind-changing effect of Martin Brennan's revelations.

46

A Rad-Trad Englishman, and an Italian

January 2002

*T*here is a way of thinking that is both idealistic and rooted in common sense. It is called radical traditionalism. It is my way of thinking and it may be yours too, but it is not likely to have any great influence in the modern world. That is because everyone in a position of power—businessmen, politicians, intellectuals, and journalists— thinks differently. And as they think, so do we all—mostly.

An inspiration and model to English rad-tradists is William Cobbett (1763–1835). Humbly born, raised as a farm boy, he educated himself to a high level and wrote in beautiful English more passionately than anyone of his time. As a radical he detested everything that we radicals still foam against—capitalism, commercialism, centralised power, and the phoney money that destroys real value and condemns honest people to poverty.

As a traditionalist Cobbett detested socialism, materialism, moralism, and schemes to improve the mentalities of the masses. His idea of progress was to look backward to the days of Merrie England under the spell of Catholic religion—when every village had its dynastic farmers and craftsmen, its sporting heroes, beauty queens, and aged wiseacres, its own customs, stories, music, style of dancing, and way of speaking.

In its ancient manor house a dimly noble family upheld the local economy and culture. Long summer days passed happily, uneventfully; midwinter was a time of fun and festival; and there was plenty of the best for all. No one had ever heard of Darwin, Freud, or Van Gogh, and no one was so clever as to have a nervous breakdown.

It comes as a shock to be reminded how closely this picture resembles the ideal images of fascism. But there is a world of difference between the gross literalism and inhumanity of a totalitarian system and the high idealism of a radical traditionalist. That difference was emphasised by Julius Evola (1898–1974), the Italian rad-trad philosopher. Though idolised by Mussolini, he was fiercely critical of the Fascist system—and of man-made systems generally. He rejected Darwin and the entirety of modern secular thinking in favour of the traditional, classical worldview. Like Socrates he perceived a divine order in Creation and he acknowledged a tradition based upon that order and passed down from the great civilisations of antiquity. The old tradition and the virtues of honesty, justice, courage, piety, and noble conduct associated with it were the main elements in Evola's reactionary revolution.

In 1951 he was arrested and brought to trial in Rome for "glorifying Fascism." The prosecutor made a farce of the proceedings by refusing to specify objectionable passages in Evola's writings, saying it was a question of his tone or "general spirit." The trial collapsed and Evola was fully acquitted.

Most of us are familiar with that sort of accusation—against one's tone, attitude, or general spirit. Bullies and witch-hunters are always on the lookout for fascism, racism, sexism, elitism, loyalism, religious sentiment, or whatever is considered most incorrect at the time. In Evola they find their ideal victim. In his most powerful book, *Revolt Against the Modern World,* he spoke of manliness, mystical sovereignty, and legitimate authority. He spoke also about occult politics and the collusions between democrats and demagogues to effeminise society and dumb it down. Inevitably, he brought in the Jews, associating the Jewish mentality with materialism. That makes him, if you like, an anti-Semite. But he was not speaking racially, nor against the Jewish tradition, which he respected. His reference was to a state of mind occurring in Jews and Gentiles alike: the state of mind that is reflected in the chaos of the modern world.

Evola was aware that his ideas were too idealistic to be practical in modern conditions. Right-wing activists called them "disabling," but he would not compromise with such would-be followers. The counter-revolution, he insisted, must happen first in the mind with the return of sanity and traditional wisdom. I go along with that. It is the old and orthodox rad-trad doctrine.

47

Bruce Chatwin's Glimpse of Truth

March 2002

*C*harles Darwin's theory is said to be the most influential product of the nineteenth century. Whose thinking, would you say, will be regarded as the twentieth-century equivalent? It is unlikely to be any of the current favourites, so here is an interesting outsider: the late Bruce Chatwin.

He was an odd character, a puritan aesthete, fastidious, with a restless mind that led him into many curious areas of knowledge. His conversation was erratic and whimsical but full of mystical insights. The deepest of these was into the essence of human nature. "We are," he said, "a nomadic species, designed with long legs for walking. At different times some of us settle down and build civilisations. But these never last. Human nature remains always the same, and it cannot forever tolerate civilised restriction. The more elaborate a society grows the more oppressive and vulnerable it becomes, and eventually it falls. Human nature reasserts itself and leads us back to our normal condition of tribal nomadism."

Our minds also are travellers. We do not remain long in one state of mind but have different moods throughout the day and year and in different ages. "That," said Chatwin, "reflects the ever-changing patterns of the wanderer's life." He pictured our natural state as a regular, ritualised journey around the sacred places of our native territory. Everything was done according to age-old custom. We received the gifts of the local spirits and responded so as to please them. Life proceeded in familiar cycles under the spell of a creation myth which we acted out in the course of our journey.

This was the primordial paradise. Its loss is allegorised in the story of the Fall and our expulsion from Eden. Yet even after we had stopped travelling, the wandering nature of the mind was allowed for in the round of feasts and festivals throughout the country. Each place had its traditional customs and music and it marked the scene of an episode in the national myth—the Arthurian saga in Celtic lands. It also represented a certain aspect of our minds and appetites. There were festivals of purity and piety, of sex and drunkenness, of trading and law-giving. At the annual festival of fools, order was abolished and outrageous behaviour was given its day. In this way human nature was allowed its full range and social restraints were made bearable.

Chatwin never published a clear statement of his thesis. The excuse he gave was that he did not want to sound didactic. But there was another, deeper reason. He was haunted by certain questions, and before he could resolve them he was diverted by literary fame. In his last book, *The Songlines,* he flirted with his great subject. But his energies were almost spent and he died without writing the book that would have made him lastingly famous.

The questions that puzzled him were these. If the nomadic life corresponds to human nature, whatever made us settle down? Whoever thought of the idea, and how did it catch on? Chatwin imagined that the first settlers were the old, the weak, and the lazy. In the course of time this element prevailed over the noble traditionalists—and from then on it was downhill all the way to hell and civilisation.

Is civilisation a nasty disease that we sometimes catch, or is it a normal, inevitable state in the cycle of history? Chatwin was inclined to take this first view. But through esoteric studies he was led toward the alchemical view—that in history, as in everything else, there is a constant progression between chaos and order. "The good news," he said, "is that human nature will outlive any system that is imposed on it." I wish he had written that book rather than his evasive "novels of ideas." It would have blown Darwin out of the water. But perhaps he knew best how to do it. He was a clever operator.

48

How Can Jesus Be God?

August 1993

*T*hough I was brought up C of E, I simply cannot understand the basis of Christianity. Jesus is the stumbling block. It was surely a great mistake by the early Christians to acclaim their prophet as God in man, as if the Ancient of Days could truly be represented by a human actor. It was blasphemous, idolatrous, and asking for trouble—which duly followed. By the second century, St. John in Patmos was guardedly denouncing the literalism of the Church and its worship of a wounded image, which he identified with the number 666, the prime symbol of imperial authority. The crucified man is an ugly image. It illustrates one side of human experience, suffering and mortification, but I cannot see it as a worthy or useful representation of God.

We Christians have often railed against the Jews for their failure to accept the divinity of Jesus, even stigmatizing them as deicides, but I now see how rightly they were guided by traditional wisdom. Jesus may well have been god-like; that epithet was applied to several great teachers in the ancient world. He may well have had priestly or shamanic powers, healing, transmuting matter, even rising from the dead. He received the word of God, spoke it fearlessly, and accepted the consequences, exemplifying the way of life which may in the long run prove the most rewarding of all. One can profit from that example and try to follow it, but if you follow a man you are following in the shadow of an image that hides the glory beyond it.

Once you establish a cult for a man and allow him to be represented by worshipful artworks you open the way to the deification of any subsequent Saviour or Liberator. London is cluttered with statues of generals and suchlike, even of the mass-murdering Bomber Harris, and some of these people actually consented to their own monumentalisation, thus making themselves publicly ridiculous. Abroad it is even worse, with butchers and tyrants brazenly displayed in vainglorious statuary. This practice began with the Romans, was continued by their Church, and flourishes almost entirely in Christian countries. In holy, iconolatrous Russia it reached its peak with the ubiquitous statues of Lenin and his sacred mummy in the Kremlin. "Sons of Lenin" was the Afghanis' name for the invading Russians. They laughed at them for worshipping a man, but that was the natural legacy of their Christian traditions.

There were many statues in the ancient world but never of actual people, usually of the dominant god or goddess of the district. Wide areas were overlooked by colossi, representing the local zodiacal influence. The gods were depicted symbolically, as ideals rather than as godlike men, and as reminders of the supreme natural powers. No one would have been so vulgar as to attempt the portrayal of God. There can be only one monument to the source of all things, the universe itself.

To see the absurdity of associating God with any man one need merely consider what is known about the Creator. Nothing at all is known because he can neither be described nor apprehended by the intellect. He is referred to, therefore, as En Soph, the unlimited. Plato in the *Parmenides* demonstrated that for every statement you make about the Ultimate, you can equally well say the opposite. Much is known about Jesus: that he was wise, compassionate, and so on, and those who invoke his spirit today say that it is as effective as ever. These are divine attributes, but no attributes at all can be ascribed to the Unlimited. Like Moses, Buddha, and Mohammed, Jesus was a holy prophet, but it cheapens the idea of Godhead to locate it in the body of a man.

PART V

Sacred Cows

49

Television, Degradation, and the Ideal

May 1993

*M*r. Major deplores violence on television. So he said, but then he backed off from the obvious corollary, that he should do something about it, muttering about the impossibility of censorship.

Of course it is not impossible to censor television. As my columnary neighbour Mr. Enfield has written, any sensible person could to it beginning with cutting out the cruelty and crudity. My own first strike would be against the coarse, vulgar, bullying, witless ruffians who call themselves comedians. It was because of them that I allowed the hire people to take back my set some years ago.

The real objection to censorship is that it does not go far enough. However many programmes you were to ban you would not get to the root of television's evil, which is the overall, insidiously degrading tone of the thing. This derives from the lugubrious, one-sided worldview which now prevails, fostered by the education system and faithfully upheld by the broadcasting authorities. Its influence is most apparent in the "serious" TV items, from the crassly politicised, trivialised news to the dollops of Darwinian propaganda doled out with the nature programmes. The violence and vulgarity are merely by-products of that established worldview, which denies the existence of true standards or principles in life, thus confining communication to the level of opinion and empiricism. If, for example, you were on a discussion programme and you dared to rise above the mock battle of opinions, seeking their reconciliation in the higher truth to which they were all aspiring, everyone would be embarrassed and you would not be invited again.

The only useful thing that can be done with television is, first, to abolish it altogether, and then to recreate it upon the basis of those ideals you wish to see active in your children and society generally. Think it through and that is the only conclusion you can come to. Television is the strongest, most pervasive influence of our times. Its power to sell any product it publicises is proved and recognised by advertisers and its cultural effect is equally potent. It moulds and sets young minds in its own image, or demonic multiplicity of images. It is a dangerous, ravening beast, the archenemy among us.

It would be quite easy to make it our best friend. Everything we wish for it can bestow upon us. Nor is it difficult to decide what to wish for. First we list the qualities which we would all like to possess and see around us, such as wisdom, a sense of justice, goodness, kindness, grace, wit, beauty, and courage. We then design our television shows to reflect and inculcate these virtues. A wise, saintly old musician, someone like Yehudi Menuhin, would know how to supervise the change of tone.

If children whine that they are bored by the classical types and harmonies which the reformed television will present to them, they can revert to the normal occupations of youth, healthy sport, bird-watching, or cycling round old churches. A free press invigorated by the high tone of its competitor will satisfy all other needs. Many people at first will object to this necessary reform; but necessary it is, for the alternative is to continue as now, allowing the chief influence upon us to be directed without scruple in the interests of personal or corporate profit. In doing so we permit the murder of ourselves and societies. Poor Mr. Major seems too confused to remedy the situation, but someone will have to make the switch from depravity to idealism, and quite soon, or we will all end up in the gutter.

50

Cannabis and the Law

October 2001

$\mathcal{T}$he first thing I read in any newspaper or journal is "Letters to the Editor." That is where you find good, honest writing and first-hand viewpoints, sometimes from people who know what they are talking about. These brief letters are far more interesting than the lengthy facetiousness of tired hacks who write "opinion" columns. The drawback is that sometimes the letters page is monopolised by a subject that does not interest me. Drugs, for instance. Every other letter for the past few months has been about cannabis, whether it is good for you or bad for you, whether it should be legalised, decriminalised, or cracked down upon.

This is a subject on which I have no particular opinion. It is every man for himself. Some people find cannabis useful. It loosens you up and distances you from yourself and your conditioned perceptions. It can provide a deeper appreciation of art and music. It helps you to see through other people's pretensions (as well as your own) and to sympathise with them. It makes you sensitive, inducing a more spiritual view of the world. Musicians, artists, and philosophers are often befriended by cannabis and liberated from base inhibitions.

On the other hand, it makes you dreamy and inactive—and cowardly too. If you're about to charge into battle, or ride in the Grand

National, the last thing you need is a relaxing smoke. It sheds an excessively clear light upon the dangers you are facing. When you want to be brave, that is the time for amphetamines—"speed," they call it. They give it to soldiers face-to-face with the enemy, and they gave it to the riot police who in 1985 smashed up the Stonehenge festival-goers. The Norse "berserkers," knights of Odin, fought or laboured invincibly under the influence of a potion with similar effects to speed. Cannabis, they would have reckoned, is for women and queers.

Every drug has its uses and equally its abuses. Cocaine provides short-term inspiration, but ultimately at the cost of one's sanity or grasp on reality. Crack is degrading but it puts you in touch with demons and awakens you to their existence. Heroin is soothing and makes you think but then deadens the brain. Ketamine takes you into the far blue yonder where you see that there is a universal source. Acid or LSD can provide the glimpse of eternity that the Pilgrim saw at the beginning of his Progress. Ecstasy makes you love and appreciate your friends and fellows. In Northern Ireland the police actively encourage the sale of Ecstasy, because at young people's raves Protestants and Catholics dance and make love together—unlike the pubs where alcohol fuels sectarian fanaticism.

The reason I am not interested in the drug debate is that the status quo seems perfectly adequate. Everyone can find what they want, and in the process they meet some very interesting people, their local drug dealers. These people are given a bad name but often they are the brightest people in the community. Youths and maidens who attend their salons are introduced to subjects which their school-teachers never touched upon. If cannabis is legalised a culture will be destroyed and many people will be thrown out of work—smugglers, gangsters, distributors, and those genteel old chaps and ladies who augment slender incomes by catering to the needs of their friends. Also out of work will be drug czars, drug squads, customs officials, and prison warders.

It is really the duty of our government to control our drug intake? As a libertarian I believe in the individual, free choice, and freedom of expression. But as a Platonist I acknowledge the right of the state to call the tune. As long as drugs remain illegal I shall respect the law but make my own private arrangements. When the law changes and you can get whatever you want from the chemist, most people who buy drugs will be those who have some creative use for them. That will finish off the "drug problem."

51
The Demon of Sex Obsession

October 1993

*T*he more we are told how tolerant and liberated we now are, the more prudish and inhibited we seem to become. A new type of crime, previously unheard of, is talked about these days. My first introduction to it was in a public park, seeing a respectable-looking gent crawling like a wounded bird beside the railings while a mob of women laid into him with handbags and pointed shoes. He had offered to buy a little girl an ice cream.

That is exactly what a character in one of my favourite childhood books has done. In *Lucy Brown and Mr. Grimes,* illustrated by Edward Ardizzone, little Lucy was treated to an ice cream by an old chap she met in the park. They were both rather lonely and pleased to have each other's company. Mrs. Brown was also pleased when Lucy invited Mr. Grimes home for tea; when he died he left his little friend all his money.

Before modern prurience put a stop to it, this sort of relationship was considered normal and praiseworthy. Every amateur of Cornish ichtheology knows the work of Richard Couch of Penzance, the great nineteenth-century expert on the mackerel and the stickleback. According to his biographer, he had two especially amiable qualities: his patience in giving up as much of his valuable time as was demanded by the blood-sucking visitors who prey on famous men, and his kindness to young people. On his nature rambles he always invited a little girl who became his "constant companion." What a charming couple, thought the old-fashioned Penzancians.

Our literary editor says I should not mention Plato any more in this column, but it is difficult to keep him out of this one. He was, of course, a paedophile, never a paederast, a lover of innocence and its firm defender against violation. So also was his teacher, Socrates, who behaved like a typical, calculating Greek when he rejected the advances of young Alcibiades. The transient beauty of youth, he said, was not a fair exchange for his eternal wisdom.

This surely is the gist of it. Young people should feel grateful and honoured if an older man takes an interest in them and is able to advance their education; and if he is affectionate toward them they should respond with propriety. In that way they can benefit their own minds and lives, while giving pleasure where it is deserved. Nowadays, woefully, innocence has been lost and the sweet friendships which arise between eager youth and wise old age are totally proscribed. Many demons are now loose in the world and the viperous devil of sexual obsession has paralysed us with its sting. No longer may the little orphan girl, the subject of so many fine paintings and poems, lead the old blind bard across trackless wastes to his next engagement. Chastity and purity are regarded as morbid aberrations and every occurrence of human love and friendship is assumed to be based on the lowest level of sexual voluptuousness.

This condition, I have heard it said, arose after the trial of Oscar Wilde, when the public first heard about the evils of sodomy, and several pairs of old friends, living together like Holmes and Watson for the convenience of sharing a housekeeper, had their windows broken. It has now gone so far that parents do not let their children play freely out of doors because they have heard about a child in some distant county who was murdered by a madman. Never one to mind my own business, I reproached a mother I know for not letting her children walk back from school by themselves along a quiet country lane. "Do you want them to be crushed by a lorry?" she asked angrily. I did not say so, but I thought it a risk well worth taking.

52
Down with School

August 1999

*F*ifty or more years ago the education we were subjected to was called classical and liberal. It was meant to encourage independent thought and the ability to see through demagogues and phoneys. That is not the sort of thing that appeals to modern governments. They could hardly co-exist with it. The old style of education was therefore denigrated, charged with elitism and religious leanings and, as far as possible, suppressed. In its place, imposed by a national syllabus, arose an ungodly concoction of low-minded materialism and misery-Marxism. If children today seem ungainly and surly it is not by nature but through education. This apparently satisfies our Government, for they have recently announced that children will enter the education process at the age of three.

A spirited attack on propagandist mass education was printed in *The Independent on Sunday* of 27 June. "Proper education," said Felipe Fernandez-Armesto, "is for the enlargement of sensibilities, the cultivation of sympathies, the sharpening of perceptions, the enhancement of life, and preparation for death—not for merely economic enrichment." And he went on, "We abuse our power over the young to engineer society and to sanctify those modern demigods, health and safety. We try to safeguard social peace by inculcating tendentious values: moral indifference and 'lifestyle-tolerance.' We misemploy schools and universities to keep children off the streets and youth out of the job market." Best of all was his last paragraph. "Universal compulsory education may be necessary, but it is a necessary evil. It has turned millions of potentially intelligent people into readers of *The Sun*. The products of compulsory schooling are the fodder of the spin-doctors and publicity wizards. Instead of making people critical, it makes them manipulable. If we abolished it, we should have a worse workforce but a better world."

The logical conclusion to this is that the world was a better place before anyone could read and write. That view is attributed in Plato's *Phaedrus* to the wise King Thamus of Egypt. When Thoth, the inventor of writing, claimed it as an aid to memory and wisdom, Thamus replied that it would have the very opposite effect, "for this invention will encourage forgetfulness in the minds of those who learn it. . . . You offer your pupils the appearance of wisdom rather than the real thing. For they will read widely but without instruction, and will seem to know much while being for the most part ignorant and troublesome, thinking themselves wise instead of being so."

The ideal which we idealists hold in mind is the greatest amount of happiness for the greatest possible number of us all. That, of course, rules out inflicting pain on children by ramming propaganda down their throats and it takes us back to happier, mediaeval days, when there was no such thing as state education. The Catholic Church provided schools and colleges where learning was accessible to those who sought and were adapted for it. Country people generally did without letters, but their cultural assets, their craftsmanship, their music and lore, their festivals, traditions, and ritualised lives were far richer than any that have been known since. The Protestant idea, to deliver the people from superstition and impel them toward rational education, was evidently misconceived, because its consequences are now apparent. Education is now a world power, greater and more influential than any other. With its proclaimed basis in atheism and egoism it is the mental tyranny that has given rise to the material tyrannies of Hitler, Stalin, Mao, and the rest that characterise the modern era. It is a kind of thought-form, a demonically controlled product of the misshapen modern mind. Like all demonic entities it reacts violently against recognition and criticism. So there is nothing much you can do except sit tight, encourage children to find their own enthusiasms, and wait for this thing to break down, as one day inevitably it will.

53

A Good Irish Education

May 1996

*T*he last people in the British Isles who received a decent education were the Irish peasants. Long before St. Patrick's time the Druid colleges of Britain and Ireland were famous throughout the ancient world and rulers in distant lands sent their children to study there. These institutions continued to flourish under Christianity, which in Celtic lands was merely a reformation of the Druid system. When the rest of the world succumbed to barbarism and Roman material-ism, missionary teachers from Ireland travelled as far as Russia and the Mediterranean, rekindling the light of culture through the doctrines of the ancient spiritual science.

According to Caesar and other authorities, the Druids taught in the style of Pythagoras, leading their pupils through number, geom-etry, musical theory, and linguistics, into the higher realms of philoso-phy and metaphysics and, finally, to the gateway of initiation. This was the climax of a twenty-year instruction period which brought those who survived it to perfect understanding and acceptance of the divine order, and thus qualified them as worthy rulers, judges, or teachers.

Every provincial Irish king was patron of a college or school of bards, where the emphasis was on genealogy (that is why the Celts are always telling you about their ancestry), legal studies, and literary composition. The medium of instruction was the Irish language and everything was learnt orally through numerically structured musical chants. Promising scholars from the poorest families were admitted free of charge. Thus in every small village high standards of piety and learning were maintained by native bards educated in astronomy, navigation, land-measurement, Greek, Latin, and the art of rhetoric.

When the old Irish colleges were suppressed by Cromwell their professors took to the road and continued to dispense education, teaching the old subjects in remote, rustic "hedge schools" for whatever their pupils could pay them. Visitors from abroad were amazed by the wit and learning of the Irish peasantry. An eighteenth-century English traveller lost in the wilds of Ireland summoned a barefoot youth who was herding goats nearby, finding that he did not speak a word of English but directed him on his way "in the Greek of Aeschylus."

To counter this irritating persistence of culture the authorities introduced compulsory education. This defeated the hedge schoolmasters and decimated the vocabulary of the Irish country folk. It also destroyed the entire meaning and purpose of education as the Druids properly perceived it. In place of the classical curriculum which instructed in the realities of life and the arts of graceful living, the new system of teaching was concerned with the trivialities of secular history and scientific empiricism. Nothing real was taught anymore. The level of popular culture is still higher in Ireland than anywhere else in Europe, but its roots have been cut through and it survives now as a memory with no living source.

The modern style of education, so called, has killed not only learning but the very idea of learning and all popular respect for it. It has produced a generation of which, according to a recent survey, almost half have no idea that the earth goes round the sun or of the time taken by that process, who despise grace and refinement, know nothing of

Latin or Greek, and communicate brutishly in a slurred jargon of about 200 words. But they are good, kind, loyal people at heart and they will produce descendants who one day, when God wills it, will be enlightened by divine knowledge, receiving the vision of paradise and reshaping our earthly institutions in accordance with it.

54

Outliving the Experts

May 1996

*A*n old chap I was talking to turned out to be a former Cabinet minister. The experience had disillusioned him. "I used to believe in science and have faith in economists," he said. "But then I discovered that these people are utterly bogus. Each one contradicts the other and none of them ever manages to be right about anything. Every year the most reputable economists produce a report on current and projected trends in the world of business, and on this document the Government bases all its financial strategies for the year. Yet every such report is invariably wrong—not just inaccurate but so far off the mark that you would do better to expect the opposite of anything the experts predict."

His final conclusion was that it was not just the economists who were always wrong but experts generally, in every department and subject. The realisation has been a great blessing to him. It has freed his mind from worry and allowed him to spend the rest of his life in classical contentment, drinking wine and gardening.

If that is a path to happiness it seems an easy one to take. The infallible wrongness of experts is a law which you can test for yourself in any subject you care to go into. My own first glimpse of it was in archaeology, where the noble artifacts of the ancients were interpreted by experts as relics of primitive superstition. This absurd view was clearly derived from Darwin's theory of evolution, and this upon examination turned out to be no more than myth, despite the experts' insistence upon its literal truth. On the most important subject of all, the origin of the world and the nature of life, the experts proclaimed certainties which changed so regularly and radically that they might just as well have said openly, "We don't know."

So it goes on. I have just read a book, *The End of the Future,* by an astute Frenchman, Jean Gimpel, recalling how life at the end of this century was predicted by experts in the 1950s and 1960s. By now, according to the highly paid prognosticators of that period, there would be no more illness or suffering. We would live to at least one hundred and fifty, taking it easy, with everything done for us by intelligent robots. Holidays would be spent on the moon or in one of our star colonies, and even the old-fashioned types who clung to Earth would be shooting around it in atomic rockets. In 1955 a thirty-minute crossing of the Atlantic was officially promised within a few years.

In actual fact, says M. Gimpel, technological progress has reached its end and the reverse has set in. Our civilisation is subject to the same laws and will follow the same cycle as all that have gone before it. Forget the experts and their babblings about time-travel through black holes and prepare for dissolution.

Gimpel's weakness, of course, is that he too is an expert and thus as inevitably fallible as his predecessors. I read his book purely for entertainment and for yet another laugh at the experts' expense. It really does make you happier when you see through these people. No longer at the mercy of their neuroses, you can develop your own view of the world, and if you are wise you will serve self-interest by making it as delightful as possible, basing it on the image of a God-given paradise, which is far truer and more lasting that the perverse imaginings of any expert.

So when people complain about modern education and how children learn nothing at all at school these days I cannot help thinking that is probably not such a bad thing after all. It took me a long time to be rid of my drummed-in fear of experts. Others in my generation never managed to work themselves free. That is why so many of them lost their money in Lloyd's.

55

A Rotten Genius

July 1992

*A*ll artists hope to influence their contemporaries and, if successful, will inevitably do so. Music is the most effective of the arts; Plato believed that it determines the future forms of government. Painters may not communicate so widely, but they certainly condition the way in which the rest of us see the world, and we are therefore entitled to remind them of their responsibilities.

Most of the artists I have met deny having any responsibilities at all. This is understandable, since the success of a modern artist has nothing to do with pleasing the public, but is gained by attracting the fancy of star-makers in the art world. At present there are no standards for judging the quality of an artist other than the opinions of modern art experts. These experts have complete licence to rig the market and it is not surprising that they do so.

The most highly praised and rewarded painter of our time was Francis Bacon, who died a few weeks ago, aged eighty-two. He was a pleasant character but eccentric, and his predilections attracted him to the low bars of Soho in the company of vicious youths and riff-raff bohemians. When drunk, sick, or overtired, he was best able to paint.

Bacon was quite unpretentious. He attuned his imagination to the abyss, and honestly, skilfully, depicted the disgusting creatures he discerned there. His art was a personal obsession and he never pretended otherwise. He would never have claimed to be "the greatest living painter" or a definitive illustrator of "the human predicament." Those things were said about him by Alan Bowness, director of the Tate Gallery in 1985, when Bacon had his exhibition there.

It must have been the most extraordinary art show ever. Gravely displayed on the walls of the national art temple was a procession of hellish beings, spattered with gore, slime, and ordure, writhing, fighting, copulating, vomiting, defecating, and screaming in torture. Some mutilated worms were enacting a crucifixion, and there was an odd creature made up of sexual parts and wearing cricket pads. A portrait of the lovely Henrietta Moraes showed her as a decomposing lump of hair and meat.

"A genius? I say Rotten!" cried Bernard Levin in the *Times*. In fifty years' time, he predicted, Bacon's pictures would be thought worthless. Meanwhile, it is our duty to discriminate in art between the true and the ugly. He was reproved by a critic who stated that it was "very old-fashioned" to consider the subject matter or content of a painting. The correct thing was to ignore the filth and concentrate on Bacon's mastery of paint and colour.

This is the exact opposite of what old Ruskin taught: that we should take the artist's technical skills for granted and judge pictures by the effect they produce on the soul. His ideal picture was "that which conveys to the spectator the greatest number of the greatest ideas."

Ruskin is certainly old-fashioned, but unaffected by fashion is the truth in what he said, that pictures influence their viewers. Bacon never thought of himself as a public figure so he never considered the public effect of his imagery. Less innocent are those who manipulated him, who established his fetid creations as official icons and made them typify "the human predicament." If one did not know that these art experts are merely vain, stupid, greedy, and thoroughly confused, one would see them as very sinister people indeed.

56
Freudian Analysis

July 1998

A painting by Lucien Freud was sold for a vast sum in New York, and the London art people complained bitterly, lamenting this great loss to the nation and reproaching the authorities for allowing it to happen. It was, they said, a disgrace to our country. I was unaffected by this wave of patriotic indignation and felt relief rather than shame at being deprived of Freud's masterpiece. We all have our weak spots and one of mine is that Freud makes me feel sick. Nothing personal, of course; it is not his character and habits but his hellish view of the world that has me retching. You cannot deny that he is a wonderfully accomplished artist, and that just makes it worse.

Freud is a confirmed literalist, painting the superficial and offering it as a true likeness. His main subject is human flesh. It is ugly stuff, and there is no harm in being reminded of that. We all have this ugliness, but we also have other aspects, and a portrait that makes no reference to these is properly called a caricature. That is Freud's own problem, you might think, but it is our problem also, because Freud is a celebrity, officially approved and widely imitated. His limited, fact-of-the-matter view of reality influences others and supports the officially promoted, low-minded worldview that is the cause of so much unhappiness today.

The moment you have said something like that you start thinking the opposite, and I am now thinking how lucky we are to have Lucien Freud, with his fine draughtsmanship and clarity of expression, still upholding standards when all around him the level of artistic communication has descended to pure gibberish. But I can't stop wondering why the dealers and curators who comprise the art establishment believe in a world of ugliness and chaos and encourage only those painters who see it that way. The answer, I think, is that these people are creeps. They are anxious to keep in step with the academic establishment, with Hawking of black hole fame, with Dawkins the zealous God-basher, with the disappointed Marxists, pandering politicians, pettifoggers, grievance-mongers, and atheistic bishops who set the tone in modern society. Instead of opposing these vulgar types by exhibitions of artistic beauty the art professionals run along with them. I suppose they have to in order to get funding.

The last thing an *Orthodox Voice* writer wants is to be heretical, but it keeps happening, and it happened again at the recent Royal Academy show of pictures from provincial galleries. They were arranged chronologically from the medieval to the modern. One reveres the ancient pictures, but their themes are mostly religious and they have little meaning to the non-specialist. The good stuff begins with the Dutch light-and-landscape painters, Jan Both, Jacob van Ruisdael, and such, and then John Constable, J. M. W. Turner, and the East Anglians. Anyone today can enjoy these and the nineteenth-century painters who succeeded them. My heresy is to regard these painters as the ultimate masters. The Americans have Frederic Church, Albert Bierstadt, and Thomas Cole, whose large canvasses exceed in splendour and beauty anything preceding them. And here we have Edwin Henry Landseer, surely the monarch (please don't laugh, just look) of English painters. Then the camera was invented and artists became "impressionists," recording their own personal impressions. After that it was downhill all the way. Many good artists such as Stanley Spencer, John Piper, and Michael Andrews gave us their honest impressions, but then the loonies and self-publicists took over, and the last exhibit in the show I saw was something like a stepladder and a tea bag, juxtaposed to represent the human dilemma. Thank God we still have Lucien Freud.

57
The Bohemian Myth

May 1992

S ometimes on a Saturday afternoon I enjoy a visit to the spacious halls of the Saatchi Gallery, hidden away off a side street in London NW. It belongs to two brothers who are said to have made their fortunes in advertising. Unkind critics have sneered at the poor Saatchis, calling their modern art collection "a load of worthless junk dumped upon them by New York art con-men." It is easy sport for such people to mock the tastes of the newly rich. The reason I go to the gallery is not to laugh but to contemplate, in a spirit of philosophic melancholy, the rare examples of human folly and credulity, which the Saatchis so piteously provide.

One wonders why they do it and who or what has persuaded them to part with hard-earned money for this rubbish. Some belief must have motivated their monstrous assemblage. It can hardly be mere greed, for there is nothing greedy in accumulating stuff that can never be resold for anything like the price given for it. It must have been some powerful faith or myth that caused the Saatchis to lose their business sense and dispose of their capital in this whimsical manner.

Yes indeed, it is a myth. The secret was revealed the other day by Jenny Blyth, Curator of the Saatchi Collection. In *The Evening Standard* she stated as follows: "Throughout history great works of art have often been derided when first created, only to be hailed as master-pieces many years later when they become our cultural icons."

We have all heard that one before. It is called the Bohemian Myth. Invented last century in Paris during the free-spirited era of *la vie bohème,* it proclaimed that any true artist was bound to suffer neglect or persecution by the coarse, unfeeling bourgeoisie. The mark of the artist was his ability to shock and scandalise these dull people. This had been the case throughout history.

The Saatchis have probably read about the Bohemian Myth in art books and romantic novels, but perhaps they have never been told that it was just a literary fancy degenerating into an excuse for self-pity, and that no serious artist has ever paid attention to it. Jenny Blyth should know that, and she would be giving better service to her employers if she quietly explained to them about the myth rather than used it to defend their lamentable collection.

She really should tell them the truth: that every artist from antiquity up to recent times has worked within the traditions of his society and has been valued according to his attainments. In the studio of his master the young painter learnt far more than the specialised techniques of his craft, and only when he had been led beyond pride in his own cleverness to acknowledge the divine source of his genius was he allowed to influence the public by exhibiting his own work.

There was no reason in the past for an artist to be rejected by his society, nor did he need to caper like a madman to attract attention. Nor are there ancient examples of great works of art which were "derided when first created, only to be hailed as masterpieces many years later"—except perhaps the Tower of Babel. Even in modern times the majority of acclaimed artists (yes, I know about Van Gogh and poor little Chatterton) have been appreciated during their working lives. All too many of them now receive instant status as "cultural icons."

If I were the Saatchi Brothers I would be inclined to instruct Jenny Blyth to sell the lot for whatever it would fetch and buy us a few decent pictures to take home.

58
Art, Money, and Revolution

December 1999

*I*n this column some years ago I commiserated with Poor Mr. Saatchi, the eminent advertiser, for having been taken advantage of by slick New York art dealers who dumped a load of complete rubbish upon him. It is what happens to rich parvenus in the art market, and fair enough. But instead of just swallowing his loss Mr. Saatchi incurred further humiliation by exhibiting the rubbish in his London gallery.

It was an embarrassing show and I felt sorry for him. Now I am not so sure. Like many people who have been swindled, Saatchi learnt the racket for himself. He sold the New York rubbish at a profit, invested in other artists and soon found himself in a position to rig the contemporary art market, making and breaking reputations by his policies of buying and selling. Now he is the biggest and most influential dealer in the country.

Yet I still feel sorry for Saatchi. It is a terrible thing to fall into the hands of the ungodly, the self-proclaimed (and proud of it) "subversives" who constitute the modern art establishment. There are only a few of them—certain dealers, curators, and critics—and, yes, they do amount to a conspiracy. If they were merely lining their own pockets at our expense it would not matter so much. But the trouble is that these

163

people are fanatically sincere. They really believe that there is no God, no truth, no standards in anything. Spontaneous individual expression is all that they value, and the only art they appreciate is that which comes from no tradition and gives rise to none. That is why they give the art prizes to buffoons.

And that is also why old values and institutions are crumbling so rapidly about us. It is no secret that the forms of art encouraged by the state affect the minds of people exposed to them. Dictators have always demanded "correctness" in art and our own great galleries were designed to instill "correct" values into the populace. Contemporary art has acquired a more powerful influence than any that came before it. Skilfully promoted in the media, exclaimed about and made provocative, it enters every mind and to some extent imprints it with a new, political form of correctness.

What sort of conspiracy is this? Can it really be that the small group in control of modern art promotion thinks it right to fill minds with obscenity, blasphemy, and garbage? Apparently so. This is a conspiracy to spread doubt and confusion, which is the classical method, as described by Dostoyevsky in *The Devils,* by which revolutionary nihilists proceed to overturn society. The art market has been rigged, not just to allow Saatchi to pile up money but for a larger, more sinister purpose—to stupefy minds and sap resistance to a revolution which is now visibly in process.

Its effects are apparent everywhere. Manly sports are officially discouraged and it is government policy to effeminise children and even the armed forces. The old, independent House of Lords has fallen and the Monarchy, once so apparently stable, is exposed as a soft target. Heaven knows what the outcome will be. A civil war seems quite possible—and in the present mood of this country it could be vicious and bloody. More probable is the appearance of a "strong leader," the popular dictator who always emerges from times of chaos.

The art manipulators are not innocents: they are clever enough to be aware of what they are doing, and they should remember the biblical saying that even though the evil must come, woe unto him through whom it cometh. If I were Saatchi I would get out of the game while still ahead, sell off the rubbish and give support to the Prince of Wales's art school, where geometry and proportion, the eternal sources of art, are taught to the discerning youths of all nations. He would find more satisfaction in that than in conspiring with creeps to exploit perverted art fads.

59
The Art of Going to Hell

January 1997

ellow guests at a friend's house in Wiltshire were a couple I called the Bourgeoisie. He was plump and rosy with that oily glow that rich men often give out; she was neurotic in the way of many rich women. They were professionally involved in modern art and it was not just their business but—in a very real sense, as we Protestants now say—their religion. They took it quite seriously and they spoke of today's fashionable artists with the reverence that was once devoted to holy saints. On a stupid impulse, or possibly to make trouble, our host showed them the little book of *Orthodox Voice* columns published last Christmas. With amiable condescension the Bourgeoisie glanced within it and I suddenly realised what was going to happen. The man's face went redder, he frowned and pointed out something to his partner. He had hit upon my article about the poor Saatchi brothers, expressing sympathy for the way they have been treated by slick international art dealers, who have made them bolster the market in rubbish and have caused the Saatchis to look foolish by exhibiting trashy art gimmicks in their pretentious gallery.

The Bourgeoisie assimilated all this in a second. I knew they were going to be angry and I also knew what they were about to say. It duly followed. My belittling of the Saatchis' artwork was a sign of uncouth ignorance. Did I not know that every great artist throughout history had been ignored by contemporaries and scorned by his generation? If people like me did not appreciate the experimental art of today that was a mark in its favour. The Bourgeoisie couple were members of the Art Elite, makers of reputations, bestowers of grants and prizes, but I was struck by the paradox that they also regarded themselves as rebels. One of their heroes was Damien Hirst, the notorious artificer of pickled livestock. Applauded and rewarded by the official institutions, he is Britain's international art star, the Gazza of our team, the Lord Leighton of our day and age. No one could be more firmly embedded in the "establishment." Yet, in the eyes of the Bourgeoisie he was a radical outsider, exciting, up-and-coming, the man to back. Only a truculent reactionary like myself could be skeptical toward his genius. They kept insisting that I was "shocked" by Hirst's manifestations, but the shock was all on their side and it was difficult to calm them down. These people have done something very clever, having their cake and eating it, dominating the art establishment and being at the same time antiestablishment progressives. It is a trick they learnt from the Marxists.

The myth they build on is of course ridiculous. Most great artists that are regarded as such today, and including that ruthless, egocentric communist, Picasso, were not neglected but held in honour during their lives.

As for Hirst, his colleagues and promoters, I was enlightened about their activities by a New York art critic who told me that the trade name for their movement is Media Art. The art does not lie in their products, which are designed for no other purpose than to attract attention, and the more cutely original they are, the more stupid and disgusting, the more they shock and scandalise the honest public, the better they serve their purpose.

It is a dirty business and those who engage in it, as artists, dealers, promoters, or curators, are thereby degraded and can never really be happy. The arts are highly influential and with that lies heavy responsibility upon those who practise them.

An artist who misuses his talents to corrupt or swindle his contemporaries is a blasphemer against the Holy Spirit. If he chooses to depict the world as chaotic and hellish he will have a corresponding experience of it, and however much praise, flattery, and riches he attracts, he will end up in hell for good and earnest.

60
A Fox's View of Foxhunting

April 1992

$\mathcal{T}$hose who are downcast by the impending triumph of the anti-hunting movement can take heart from a remarkable prophecy uttered by a wise fox near Guiting Wood, Gloucestershire, in 1871. The man who heard it was Tom Hill of the Berkeley Hunt. He had become separated from his hounds and as he sat listening for their sound he was addressed by a venerable, silver-coated fox. Tom Hill said that it was like a dream, but he saw and heard the fox clearly and he was able to remember the gist of what it said. The prophecy was transposed into verse—following the correct tradition of Macpherson's Ossian—and was published as a little book, bound in scarlet cloth, by the Duke of Beaufort.

Not surprisingly for one so wise, the fox was passionately in favour of fox-hunting and spoke of all the benefits and privileges it had brought to his race. Yet he foresaw that hunting, with all other good old English ways and customs, would eventually be abolished. Then would come an age of misery, with atheism taught in schools, materialism established in philosophy, usury condoned by Church and state, and systematic cruelty to animals. The fox predicted the Common Market, which he bluntly described as a surrender of our national independence to a dictatorship of European financiers, the prevalence of the godless metric system, the decline of manliness, and the loss to Englishwomen of their sweet femininity. These are some of the many verses in which his words are perpetuated:

> *No word of prayer, no hymn of praise,*
> *Sound in the village school;*
> *The people's education*
> *Utilitarians rule.*

> *The homes where love and peace should dwell*
> *Fierce politics shall vex,*
> *And unsexed woman strive to prove*
> *Herself the coarser sex.*

> *Mechanics in their workshops*
> *Affairs of state decide;*
> *Honour and Truth, old-fashioned words,*
> *The noisy mobs deride.*

> *The statesmen that should rule the realm*
> *Coarse demagogues displace;*
> *The glory of a thousand years*
> *Shall end in foul disgrace.*

All these things can be said to have come to pass, and it cannot be long before the outlawing of hunting sets the seal on the fox's prophecy and confirms its 100 percent accuracy.

This makes credible the second part of the utterance, where the fox tells of an eventual restoration. One day, he says, the English people will cast down the golden calf, throw off their subservience to greed and commerce and return to their ancient, God-given traditions and institutions. Happy children shall raise once more the maypole on the green, and:

Again the smiling hedgerow
Shall field from field divide.
Again among the woodlands
The scarlet troop shall ride.

My own views on hunting are based entirely on the fox's prophecy. You can ban it, but you can never dig out its roots in human nature and culture. There is a long tradition of oracular sayings by hunted beasts, but whoever heard of a prophecy from a broiler chicken? And no one ever makes pictures or poems about vermin-control officers.

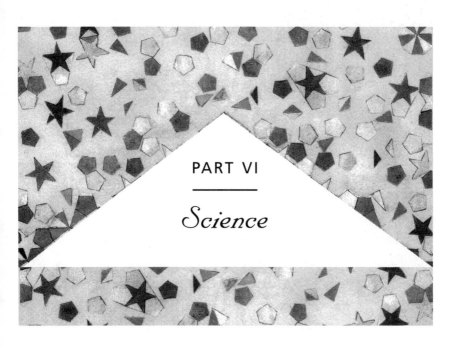

PART VI

Science

61

The Missing Link Fantasy

November 1994

*A*lerted by that curious and original writer Roy Kerridge, I visited the Natural History Museum to see its propaganda display on behalf of Darwin's theory of evolution. "We all belong to the ape family," cried a large notice, followed by an invitation to inspect the evidence. This turned out to be the same as ever, some fragmentary fossils of ancient ape bones together with evolutionists' "reconstructions." These reconstructions are fascinating. When you go into the subject and discover how the same data is interpreted by rival experts to produce entirely different looking creatures, you see for yourself how arbitrarily the whole business is conducted. The bits of bone fossil tell almost nothing about the appearance of the creatures they came from, whether they were furry or bare-skinned, whether their noses were prominent or ape-like. What we see in these propaganda shows are various depictions of the "missing link" fantasy, to some of which the evolutionists have wistfully given human names, Lucy and so on.

Soon after my visit to the museum, the newspapers were suddenly full of "Missing Link Found" headlines, sparked off by an article in *Nature* about a new set of fossil bones discovered in Ethiopia. Editorials triumphalised about the vindication of Darwin. There was a tone of relief in the articles that surprised me, because evolutionists' textbooks have long declared that no further proof is needed of our common ancestry with apes. Apparently they had not been so certain after all—until now.

This whole nonsense was gloriously debunked on the front page of *The Independent*. Below a photograph of an ape with her baby, walking upright and carrying a stick, the article began, "The missing link is alive and well and living with her family and friends in a Warwickshire zoo." The ape was a bonobo, a kind of chimpanzee from west central Africa. It is said to be "very similar" to the sensational new missing link. The bonobo has certain characteristics in common with humans, such as its way of walking and its wide vocal range, but it is unmistakably an ape, and all the new fossil evidence proves is that it has been around, virtually in the same form, for at least 4.5 million years.

The reason I keep gnawing away at the old bone of evolutionism is because of the dreadful effects it has on our minds and societies. In a period which has dedicated itself to the eradication of racism it is amazing that it is still officially fostered. Until quite recently the biology museum at Princeton University, the model for many others, had a "rise of man" display showing through a series of figures how the original shambling ape began to stiffen its backbone, stood erect as a Negro, and finally evolved into a White Man. That tableau, though now discreetly remoulded, still remains a popular and potent image. That is why it is considered such a deadly insult to liken a black man to a monkey.

Like all other creatures of earth, human beings are shaped by the genius of their native territory—its tone, temperament, rhythm, and colour. The range of human types is so wide that an alien evolutionist would probably imagine that they were each evolving into a separate species. To correct that, the classical, orthodox view is that each of the conventionally numbered twelve races of mankind contributes its particular note to the chorus in praise of the Creator, the source of our common humanity. Roy Kerridge pointed out that the Natural History Museum was designed like a cathedral to display the entire range of the Creator's handiwork. Now, as you can see, it is firmly in the hands of the evolutionists.

62

Darwin and the Damage

November 1997

*I*t is time to have another go at Darwin's pernicious theory of evolution and to remind ourselves of how much damage it has done in shaping the modern world. The theory itself has lost much of its credibility. All professors of the life sciences pay lip-service to Darwinism—they have to, or they would lose their posts—but most of them find it so unrealistic, so incompatible with the processes of nature they actually observe, that they quietly ignore it. The only active defenders of Darwin are fundamentalist zealots such as Richard Dawkins, a clever young man who is in a phase of rejecting God and preaching materialism. May God save him and make him happy.

I was brought back to this subject by writing an article on feng shui, that superstitious farrago as it now is, which was a state science in pre-modern China and was responsible for the harmonious aspect and social order of the traditional Chinese landscape. Because of feng shui, the Chinese, both the people and the authorities, opposed and frustrated the rational schemes of Western businessmen to desecrate their countryside with factories, mines, and railways. To oppose feng shui, the businessmen called in the missionaries. Their reasoning was that Jesus said nothing about railways and industry; Christianity has nothing against them, so if the Chinese could be made Christian they would have no further objection to the despoliation of their land by foreign enterprises. From the 1860s Church of England clergymen flooded into China. They all knew their Darwin, and his *Origin of Species* gave scientific sanction to their mission. White man's science had discovered the origin of the nature of life, and it was the white man's destiny to proclaim those discoveries to the other races, together with modern-minded Protestantism. Jesus and Darwin in partnership were a formidable team.

The nations of Asia and Africa have suffered terribly from European delusions, but the worst-hit victim of his own propaganda is the white man himself. In Britain, Darwin is our culture-hero, far more respected and protected from criticism than old King Arthur or the reigning Queen. Darwinism is the central pillar of the Western scientific worldview, and wherever materialism has prevailed—in Soviet Russia and even, after many wars and revolutions, in China—Darwinism has been established as a state science. Yet the whole edifice is based upon ignorance, cultish faith, and outright fraud. The ignorance is excusable; Darwin had no idea that the fossil record, virtually unexplored in his time, would contradict his thesis of gradual evolution. And one can understand how scientific materialism can develop, as in the case of Dawkins, into a quasi-religious faith.

Less easily forgivable are the fraudulence and sharp practice with which Darwinism was established. To those who would seriously like to investigate it, I recommend Gertrude Himmelfarb's *Darwin and the Darwinian Revolution*. The most successful evolutionists' hoax was the Piltdown Man, which converted many waverers to their faith. Another, exposed in *The Times* on 11 August, was Haeckel's trick of pretending through falsified drawings that the embryo of every species repeats its evolutionary history. The downfall of science is that it is confronted with the law of supply and demand. If evidence of evolution is required, and therefore valuable, there are always people to provide it.

I am uncertain about how life began, how it developed, and where it is going, but I am quite sure that scientists also are ignorant on these matters. That is why I am uninhibited in praising God my Creator, the source of all the delights I experience in this world, and feel greatly superior to the poor Chinese communist who has been crippled by materialism. But that is the way we white men think.

63

The State Myth

May 1992

*O*f all the subjects I have ever written about, the one which always brings the liveliest response is anti-Darwinism. Distinguished professors write letters of protest, showing their complete ignorance about the nature of the Darwinian Myth, why it is basically untrue and why it is philosophically objectionable. I was not surprised therefore, but naturally gratified, when some skeptical remarks about Darwinism included in my first column attracted a letter from a leading evolutionist, Professor Richard Dawkins, reproving me for having insulted his faith.

Now I am no Salman Rushdie, and if Richard Dawkins chooses to worship the goddess of Chance with Darwin as a holy prophet, I do not care to upset him. If he and his circle were content with celebrating their materialism as a personal cult one could be benevolently tolerant. It is when they try to force their beliefs on everyone else—using the education system, the BBC, and their own powers of invective to fortify their propaganda—that one simply has to draw the line. What really is the status of Darwinism? It is, proclaims Dawkins, TRUE (his capitals) and by so proclaiming he reveals it as a matter of belief. So let us speak plainly about this: Darwinism is a secular faith, elevated to the rank of State Myth and upheld with religious intensity by the scientific high priests of materialism. It has no foundation in either true science or true philosophy.

Like other brands of religionists the Darwinians exhibit ancient bones as evidence of their fables. We Protestants are supposed to abjure the cult of holy relics, but I enjoy seeing these bones and would not dream of laughing at them in the presence of the faithful—even though many of them are outright forgeries and all they illustrate is credulity and wishful thinking. I particularly enjoy the imaginary types of men and beasts which are fabricated from the old bone fragments. Best of all is when two rival evolutionists use the same fragments to draw up two completely different creatures.

The most persuasive relic the evolutionists ever had was the famous skull of the Sussex ape-man, "Piltdown Man," constructed by unknown evolutionists in 1912 and presented in their textbooks as the earliest human type. I liked it for showing that the first man was English (a point rubbed in by the hoaxers who planted a fossil object shaped like a cricket bat alongside it). Other Englishmen liked it too, and we venerated it for forty years until some jealous foreigner exposed it. By that time it had done its job, stilling doubts about evolution and finally converting the waverers.

I should like to go on and be sarcastic about other Darwinian relics, such as the notorious Archaeopteryx, the supposed halfway-house between reptiles and birds, which Fred Hoyle in 1986 proved to be a fake. More important, I should like to dwell upon the political consequences of Darwinism, its effect on the European mind, and its part in the development of racial theories and episodes of genocide. Since, however, Darwinism is just a matter of opinion, it is best dealt with on its own level by quoting another opinion by another distinguished professor. The odds against life having evolved by blind chance, says Prof. Chandra Wickramasinghe, are about the same as the odds against a whirlwind blowing through a scrap-yard and assembling a perfect Boeing 747. I much prefer this analogy to the confusing one about limitless monkeys and their typewriters.

64
Stopping the Unstoppable
October 1999

*T*he Americans have been in my good books lately. First they have aborted attempts at bringing in metrication, and second, some of their school authorities have banned the theory of evolution from being taught as scientific fact. The Americans may have their little faults, but the United States rest on a bedrock of religion and common sense which in Europe has been eroded. That is why they can do things that we would never dare to—for fear of our atheistic majority.

That majority, highly represented in the press, responded furiously to the Creationists' victory in Kansas. Everyone deplored it, and *The Telegraph* put up a dour Darwinian, Steve Jones, to reaffirm the evolutionists' faith. Yet that newspaper has a religious correspondent, Clifford Longley, who writes on Fridays. He has been doing it for years, and I have never been particularly interested. But suddenly he has become inspired. His breakthrough came when he discovered the Anthropic principle. The atheists have been trying to hide it from us for years, but cosmologists have shown that the odds against the universe, life, and consciousness having arisen by blind chance are so many billions of billions to one that there is no reasonable argument against the acceptance of divine creation. Implied by the Anthropic principle is that our world has been specially and ideally designed. Longley chided the atheists for not accepting the logic of their own science. Then the following week he took on the evolutionists.

As a veteran campaigner against the dreary, demoralizing worldview of evolutionism, I feel qualified to recommend Longley's *Telegraph* column of 27 August as the most radical, outspoken brief critique of the evolutionists' faith that I have ever read. Darwin's theory was confined to biology, but Herbert Spencer and other socialists made "the survival of the fittest" into a paradigm of life generally. This gave pseudo-scientific justification to raw capitalism, state monopolizing, racial superiority theories, genocide, godless behaviour, and all the major plagues of the twentieth century.

And that is merely the superficial damage. The amount of pain and suffering that evolutionist thinking has inflicted on individual minds is too great to contemplate. Longley concluded that the theory of evolution should be allowed in schools, but that it should be "subjected to the most rigorous deconstruction imaginable." Perhaps, he said, "it should become part of the new fashion for Holocaust studies as a warning of what bad science is really capable of." That is strong talk, necessarily so for Longley to make his point: that Darwin's idea was hijacked by atheists, promoted from a theory to a dogma, and made the cornerstone of a new, godless faith that values nothing except scientific progress. It is in Darwin's name, says Longley, that scientists claim genetic engineering to be inevitable. You cannot stop progress is their creed, as it was to the eugenics professors in Hitler's time.

These people are everywhere, setting up progress and novelty as the first principle in art, religion, philosophy, and other inappropriate fields—not with evil intent but because they recognise no higher values. They will not get away with it, of course, because human nature yearns for truth and divine order and will not long put up with any man-made system of tyranny. It is perceptive of the Americans to reject the metric system along with Darwinian education. The metre also is an atheistic device. Unlike the foot it has no inherent meaning, and it is the only unit of measure worldwide that does not relate equally to the dimensions of the earth, to the human frame, and to a certain unified code of number that was the basis of all the traditional sciences.

These are deep waters and I keep getting into them. To speak plainly, let us be suspicious of anything that is said to be progressive, or unstoppable, or even good for you. It is almost bound to be a racket.

65

Too Noisy and Violent

April 1993

S tartling news was splashed across the front pages of *The Independent* and other papers one day last April. Scientists had finally proved the Big Bang theory of cosmology, thereby solving the question of how the world began. So carried away were the scientists by this alleged triumph that one of them likened it to the discovery of the Holy Grail.

My first reaction to this fatuous hyperbole was that someone wanted to renew his research grant and it was therefore necessary to trumpet some good news. According to a new book I had been reading, *The Big Bang Never Happened,* by an astute American, Eric Lerner, the Big Bang theory is in serious trouble. There is no empirical evidence to support it, and it has failed every observational test. So the Big Bang people feel threatened. No wonder they had to grab the headlines.

The notion that a pinhead or Ping-Pong ball suddenly exploded and then spontaneously generated life and consciousness is one of those explanations, which, as Charles Fort used to say, itself requires explanation. Who or what made this pinhead and packed a whole universe into it? When was it made, and where, and why did it go off like that? Scientists are properly scornful of these questions, implying that only idiots or mischief-makers would ask such things. So we shut up and hide behind Mr. Lerner.

His notion is that the universe had no beginning and will never come to an end. It is limitless, going on forever, and beyond it there is nothing—not even Nothingness itself. His main authority for this belief is the "plasma cosmologist," Hannes Alfven of Sweden, whose influence is prevailing in many branches of science, sapping the world-view of the Big Bang advocates.

This sounds equally incredible. But Mr. Lerner at least has the wit to see that cosmology is no cut-and-dried scientific matter, and that the images of the world it proposes are largely subjective. There have always been people like him whose temperaments incline them toward an infinite universe, while those of another cast of mind prefer a limited, mathematically rational model with a proper beginning and end. It is safe to say that neither side will ever triumph permanently over the other. One need not be a high-grade mystic to perceive how the universe adapts itself to our view of it. In studying its nature we are actually studying ourselves—a subject—which is endless and irresoluble.

Those who professionally dream up universes should recognise their responsibilities to the rest of us and consider the social and aesthetic qualities of their mental creations. After all, it is we who have to live in them. The Big Bang is too noisy and violent, and I prefer the corresponding New Testament image of the tiny mustard seed, which exploded into the world tree, attracting life and spirit. For official use, a suitable creation myth is Plato's "likely account" of a benevolent Creator who made the best possible universe as a reflection of his own ideal state and animated it with a soul, constituted as a scale of music. A story on those lines satisfies the cosmological needs of children and simple folk, and Plato's mathematics of creation have kept generations of scholars happily bemused ever since. Yet esoterically, in the *Parmenides,* he acknowledged that the world partakes of both limit and infinity; it can never be codified, and the only access to its secrets lies in the enlightened mind. Nevertheless, we still need the "likely account," and none of the modern cosmologists I have heard about seem capable of providing it.

66

Collisions with God

April 1993

Now that *The Guardian* has largely got rid of the whingeing women and moaning Marxists who used to monopolise its columns, I have taken to reading it and have enjoyed some interesting articles. There was one the other day warning governments around the world about a dangerously brilliant genius called Steven Weinberg, who is looking for six billion pounds and a large part of a country to use for building a "superconducting supercollider." It is a wide steel tube, precisely made and forming a ring fifty-three miles in diameter, in which protons are to be whizzed around at almost the speed of light. They will collide with other protons, smashing them into thousands of bits which will be studied by battleship-sized computers. This, says Weinberg, will tell us how the universe was made and prove it to be governed by laws "of a quite impersonal kind." It will also prove it to be purposeless and pointless, and the effect will be to create a renaissance of human spirit and civilisation.

It may be that the Tower of Babel caused such a renaissance in its time, but the record is that it made people argue in a thousand different tongues before collapsing in ruins. This seems quite likely to happen to Weinberg's machine. It is to be powered by 3,840 huge magnets and 888 smaller ones, any of which, if imperfectly designed, will tear the thing apart. Obviously one should not stand too near it, especially since its ultimate purpose is to discredit the notion of God. Strangely enough, President Bush, who called himself a defender of Christian values, wanted it built in America.

Not that God has much to fear from this hubristic contrivance. The task for which it is specially designed is to look for the hypothetical Higgs Boson, a fragmentary particle that exists for less than a hundred billion billionth of a second! This is so short that even the battleship computers could never record it, but Weinberg hopes to see evidence of it in "the decay products of its decay products." Even if he does so, or thinks he has done so, the ephemeral Higgs Boson seems but a modest rival to the eternal Deity.

A few weeks later *The Guardian* brought tidings from physics professor Ian Barbour of Minnesota, who has discovered that the universe bears the unmistakable print of its Creator. If its rate of expansion had been a fraction of a million millionth part smaller, it would have collapsed, and if it had been a millionth part greater it would not have allowed stars to form. Moreover, if the structure of atoms, the human brain, and other essentials were produced by chance, it was in defiance of odds amounting to many billions-to-one against. There are more connected synapses in the brain, he declared, than the number of atoms in the universe. Had there been just one slight deviation in the cosmic scheme, it would have fallen to pieces like Mr. Weinberg's magnets.

Perhaps these two professors, each in his own way, is trying to say the same thing, for I observe that Weinberg's machine is kabbalistically designed to express the various names and numbers of God. Both 3,840 and 888 are important symbolic numbers, the latter being the esoteric number of the name Jesus. A simple prayer wheel, computer-driven perhaps, might be just as effective and far less dangerous and expensive than the supercolliding contraption.

Mr. Weinberg is certainly very clever, but cleverness is like good looks—an asset which if wrongly directed can be the ruin of oneself and others. Thomas Taylor the Platonist displayed the correct order of values in criticizing Newton's mechanical theory of the universe as "good mathematics but bad philosophy."

67

A Shiver of Cold Fusion

January 1995

*I*n 1959 C. G. Jung published his most prophetic book, *Flying Saucers: The Myth of Things Seen in the Sky*. These apparitions, he said, coinciding with the end of an astrological age, are portents of a radical change in the world-order and of a corresponding change in our overall way of thinking. Many of Jung's followers, straining for respectability, did not like this book; it made no concessions to New Age fantasies of a sudden peace-&-love outbreak, but predicted a series of upheavals so strange and unexpected that Jung was concerned for the mental balance of those caught unprepared for them.

The most dramatic event of our lifetimes has been the collapse of the Soviet Union and the cruel sham of communism. None of the experts foresaw its imminence, nor did they foresee the sudden ascendancy of religious fundamentalism in Iran, for such abrupt turns in the current of affairs are rationally unpredictable. The turn of a tide is not immediately felt, but it is now increasingly obvious that a complete reversal has taken place, and events are now moving in the opposite direction from the course they have followed during the whole modern era.

The fall of the Berlin Wall was just one effect of this change.

Others are sure to follow, bringing down established institutions and systems of thought, and one of the earliest victims of the process seems likely to be modern science. Like the communist political system to which it is closely related, modern science is a corrupt, unrealistic, and therefore extremely dangerous institution, not just in its practices but in its basic outlook. It constitutes an effective tyranny, maintained by ruthless suppression of all data that contradict its materialistic assumptions. Some of its ignoble activities have previously been detailed in this column; one of the latest is the scandal of cold fusion research.

The discovery of cold fusion, first announced about five years ago, is in effect the rediscovery of alchemy, for it involves the transmutation of elements. By some unknown process, hydrogen isotopes become fused at room temperature and produce "free" energy. The implication is of an unlimited source of water-derived power, cheaply and universally obtainable, requiring no elaborate technology and causing no pollution, despoliation, or radioactive waste.

In one of the few scientific magazines I subscribe to, *Frontier Perspectives* published at Temple University, Pennsylvania, is an account of the determined efforts by the high priests of science to suppress cold fusion research while vilifying and traducing its proponents. *FP* names some of the highly placed guilty people, but I shall not repeat their names here because, like Judas, they are merely fulfilling their unfortunate destinies. The authorities of science are bound to resist alchemy, just as the Vatican is bound to resist contraception (though giving way on usury and evolutionism). Their punishment will be the mockery of future historians.

Cold fusion has now been performed in laboratories all over the world, and the evidence for it has become irresistible. In other related fields, parapsychology for example, experiments under scientific conditions have destroyed the foundations of the scientific worldview. The whole monstrous idol will one day come toppling down, and that will be a day of liberation. But it is not a day I personally look forward to. The fall of the Berlin Wall was a disaster for many people, and the fall of the scientific world-order will be a terrible experience for those of us who are utterly dependent upon it.

*What has happened
to time? Why is there now so little of it
compared to the amount there used to be?
into those*

68

The Agribusiness Racket

July 2000

hat's the way a Scotsman always reasons," roared William Cobbett when he came across Adam Smith's theory of economics. "He reckons the wealth of a country by the amount the government takes out of it." Its actual wealth is the amount retained by its inhabitants; but Smith's way of thinking has prevailed not just among Scotsmen but throughout the whole Western world. One of its products is the chemical agribusiness, which is not only a mighty money-maker but sees itself as the saviour of mankind. I happened to hear one of its bosses being criticised for his involvement in the genetic engineering racket. The man looked miserable, shrugged and said, "But we do have to feed the world." I did not have the heart to argue but wished that old Cobbett had been there to deal with him.

Someone who would have done just as well is Dr. Vandana Shiva who gave one of the Reith Lectures this year. She has seen for herself in her native Punjab the catastrophic effects of big-business, chemical agriculture on the fertility, wealth, culture, and happiness of the rural population. She tells of plagues, droughts, and famines; of sterile fields, barren trees, and poisoned waters; of desperate, debt-ridden farmers driven to suicide or, with their families, into city slums. Country districts, once populous and self-supporting, have become deserts. It is not, she emphasises, a natural disaster but entirely and systematically man-made. And at the root of it is the method of accountancy pioneered by that cold Scotsman, which gives value only to goods and products than can be marketed for cash, and attributes nothing to the crafts and husbandry of traditional human life. Smith's disdain for the peasant and the independent rural economy, assimilated by both Marx and capitalism, is now openly and mercilessly expressed. Anything hand-made, says Dr. Shiva, is looked down upon or rejected as a "health hazard." Anyone who is not contributing money to the national economy, who is merely living well in his or her local community, owing nothing to any man, growing one's own crops for one's own favourite dishes, repeating one's own songs and dances at one's own traditional festivals; that person is now evaluated as a "superfluous unit," an "enemy of the people," and finally a "fascist." That is the name that Stalin smeared onto the Ukrainian peasants before he obliterated their culture.

I rejoiced in Dr. Shiva's lecture and made copies to send to friends. But I did not realise how powerful it was until I saw the reactions to it. Journalists called her a hysteric, a hippy, even a man-hater. I was not surprised to see Matt Ridley (well known to readers of this column as the man who infallibly grasps the wrong end of every stick) pouring scorn upon her as an enemy of progress. That is a sure sign that she is right. But I do see that there are two sides to this question. If you believe with Ridley that a global system of chemical agriculture with genetically engineered plants and animals is the only practical option, you may feel sorry for the poor Asian and African country people, but you will conclude regretfully that there is no place for them in the modern world. That is how evolutionists a century ago rationalised the exterminations of aboriginals.

Two centuries ago Cobbett made a survey of Horton Heath in Hampshire. It was a scruffy common fringed with dwellings and supporting some 200 people on its 150 acres. By economists' reckoning it was a valueless waste. But when Cobbett counted up the animals that grazed on it and the various products of its cottage gardens, he found that it yielded much more than a commercial farm of similar acreage. Dr. Shiva says the same thing, that "small biodiverse farms can produce thousands of times more food than the large, industrial monocultures," and in far happier and healthier conditions. I think she is that prophet long awaited by us radical traditionalists, the new Cobbett, just as bold and more likely to be effective.

69

How Talking Began

September 1996

*B*ruce Chatwin used to say that language began with people singing as they walked. But then he would. This is a great subject for crank theories. The French Academicians in the nineteenth century heard so many of them that they declared the subject a waste of time and banned further discussion. Originally, according to the Bible, "the whole earth was of one language and of one speech"; diversity of tongues came later as God's way of halting the construction programme at Babel. That implies all languages derive from a common prototype, and much effort has been given to identifying the *Ursprache*. Hebrew, Gothic, Sanskrit, Welsh, Basque, and others have been claimed as the language which God first gave to Man and which he presumably speaks himself. Early studies of wild people and children raised by beasts were largely to do with identifying their animal cries as components of the natural language.

For orthodoxy on such a weighty subject one turns, of course, to Plato, and finds it in one of his strangest and least-known books, *Cratylus*. Subtitled *On the Correctness of Names,* it consists of a debate between Socrates and two others, one of whom claims that there is an art in naming. The other disputes that and says that names are arbitrary and points out that foreigners name everything quite differently from the Greeks. Socrates tells them that there is indeed an art of naming. Every name is a "vocal imitation" of the thing it describes, and is made up from a selection of sounds, later represented by letters, each of which has its inherent character and meaning. The poets or name-givers of each nation produce widely different results through their imitations, but these are no more different than would be expected from a group of artists each painting the same landscape.

The part that attracted my attention was where Socrates gives examples of sounds with particular meanings. "R," he says, conveys rush, hurry, rapid, running. "L" is a sleek glide or slow flow, and "G" is another kind of motion, sluggish and glutinous. He was speaking, of course, in Greek, and the fact that his characterisations of sounds apply equally well to English seemed to prove his point. So I went further into the matter, discerned the meaning of each letter, and published *Euphonics: A Poet's Dictionary of Sounds*—enjoyable to do and rewarding in every way except that no one reviewed or bought it.

Some letters are actually shaped in accordance with their meaning. "S" is sibilant and looks serpentine ("Piss off, you slimy snake," she hissed); "B" with its two bulges is applied to similarly shaped parts of the body—breasts, boobs, bum, buttocks, bollocks—and, when cheeks are blown out, is heard in bullying boasts, brags and bluster; "F" looks and is frivolous; the priapic "P" sounds pompous and important as in: Papa the President proudly parades his troops past the imperial palace. In no dialect could a word such as whimper ever mean bellow. Illustrating that point, a rare writer on this subject, American philosopher Benjamin Blood, declared that you could not possibly call a tub an icicle, or vice versa.

In the language of the gods everything has its ideal name. "That language," said Socrates, "is beyond human ken or utterance," but despite the inadequacies of our name-givers it influences every word we use. So language comes from imitation, beginning perhaps with something uncontroversial, such as naming the cuckoo. The more expressive a language is, the better it is adapted to survive, and that is to the advantage of blunt, alliterative Anglo-Saxon. No wonder English is such a popular language. Next time you hear yobs howling in the street, try believing their roars and wails are spontaneous attempts at rediscovering the primordial speech of the gods.

70

Who Settled America?

June 1992

$\mathcal{I}$'ve just had a letter bearing a US postage stamp showing a group of Indians on a rock with the legend, THE FIRST AMERICANS CROSSED OVER FROM ASIA. I gratefully added it to my Propaganda Stamp Album, wherein are many other examples of someone's political or academic theory officially proclaimed as fact.

This new stamp was no doubt meant kindly—to make the recent Vietnamese immigrants feel more at home perhaps. Yet if I were an American Negro, Jew, Arab, or Paleface, I would ask the Post Office to do justice by issuing another stamp proclaiming my ancestors as the New World pioneers. And if I were an American Indian I would insist on a stamp which said that we came from nowhere but America and had been there from the beginning. I would then seek recognition for a thesis, which many scholars have upheld, that my people brought the light of culture to the entire ancient world. I would conclude, following the learned W. S. Blacket (*The Lost Histories of America,* 1983), that "the Apalachian Indians with their priests and medicine men must have been the builders of Stonehenge."

The oldest known artifacts in North America were dated by the renowned archaeologist Louis Leakey to as early as 100,000 BC, so there is no saying where or whence the first American arose. On the other hand, there is much published evidence of pre-Columbian voyages to America from West Africa, Egypt, Palestine, Scandinavia, Britain, and other countries, implying that ocean travelling was far more widespread in antiquity than modern conventions allow. If one has the sort of mentality that likes to believe something, there is the largest possible choice of theories about who was the first American. The one I favour—for reasons not unconnected with my grandmother, Mary Ann Evans of Glamorgan—is that the best if not the first Americans were those Welsh-speaking Indians whose kindness, courtesy, and perfect command of the Celtic idiom impressed generations of European settlers.

From 1608, when Captain Wynne was employed by English businessmen to interpret the Celtic speech of the West Virginia Indians, up to the nineteenth century, the Welsh language appears to have been the common means of communication between the colonists and the natives. It often dissolved misunderstandings and even saved people's lives. Francis Lewis, who signed the Declaration of Independence, was freed by his Indian captors in 1757 after he spoke to them in Welsh, and the Rev. Morgan Jones was similarly spared. In 1685 he was arrested by Tuscarora Indians, charged with illegal preaching, and sentenced to death. Allowed to say a last prayer, he addressed his Maker out loud in his native Welsh. The Indians were delighted to hear someone speaking their language. They forgave Mr. Jones, and he remained with them for several months, edifying the tribe thrice weekly with his sermons.

The explanation for the Welsh Indians is that they were descendants of the 300-strong colony planted in America by Prince Madoc of Wales in the twelfth century. This is no less plausible than the rival legends that America was discovered by Columbus or the Vikings, and there is more evidence of the existence of Welsh Indians than for the official pronouncement that the first Americans were from Asia. I look forward to the day a US postage stamp shows dark-visaged Native Americans with the inscription, THEY CAME FROM WALES.

71

Geller, Adler, and Beyond

July 1994

ife is famous for being a funny thing, but I never thought mine could possibly lead me into trouble with Larry Adler. He is, I know, a very talented and, they say, a most amusing and liberal-minded person, so the last thing I had expected was to end up in his bad books. But unfortunately I stirred up a bee in his bonnet and he is angry with me. The reason is that he thinks I am a believer, and an opposite believer to himself. If he were a reader of this column (although why should he be?) he would understand that I hold to no fixed beliefs and know nothing for certain about any subject whatever. Least of all do I know anything about Uri Geller.

Yet Mr. Adler has accused me of believing in Geller's alleged magical powers. The cause of this misunderstanding is that in an *Oldie* review of Richard Milton's book exposing the science racket, I quoted his remark that Geller's "powers" have passed all of the laboratory tests applied to them. To me, not being a believer in empirical science, this means very little. To Adler, who is just such a believer, it ought to be significant. Yet in this case he rejects science and calls for Geller to be investigated by stage magicians.

This throws everything into the usual state of confusion, for if stage magicians are the best investigators of Geller, they might just as well look into other alleged phenomena. An obvious case for them is the Americans' claim that they sent a man to walk on the moon. This is widely believed in the Western world, but most people in the East, including the philosophers, are highly skeptical. They too have seen *Star Wars* and other productions of the Hollywood magicians, and have observed how easily they can reproduce the effects claimed by rocket scientists.

I do not altogether disbelieve the American rocket, and my attitude to Geller is much the same. He may have unusual powers, exercising mind over matter; he may be a fraudulent conjuror, or perhaps he is a bit of both. That last suggestion sounds weak, but it gains prominence as one reads the voluminous records of the Society for Psychical Research (SPR). For almost a hundred years now these worthy folk have skeptically, by scientific methodology, investigated mediums, mentalists, and purveyors of witchcraft generally. Most cases have been dismissed as trickery or delusion, but some have continued to defy rational explanation.

Some people have repeatedly been able, under conditions which seemed to eliminate all possibility of fraud, to manifest or move objects, predict the fall of dice, and do other things that modern science deems impossible. Yet on other occasions some of these same people have been caught up in blatant trickery. According to Ralph Noyes, Honourable Secretary to the SPR, mediums will often cheat when they think they can get away with it, while in rigorous tests they prove themselves genuine. The Society, he claims, has documented evidence of psychic powers which, if it supported an orthodox scientific theory, would be accepted without question. Yet, fearing for their reputations, scientists turn their back on it.

With so many serious matters to discuss, it may seem a waste of a column to write about Uri Geller. But I have a soft spot for Larry Adler and would like to help him. My best advice to him is to accept the data of our existence, the world of actual human experience, and not impose theories and systems of belief upon it. He should not expect it to be rational, consistent, or explicable. This will make him happier, less fretful, and just as good a man as, they say, he has always been.

72
Don't Worry,
It's All Taken Care Of

June 1998

*I*t is not that I want to add to anyone's worries—quite the opposite. It is purely in my trying-to-be-helpful mode that I draw attention to a source of worry that can be with you all your life and overshadow it to the end, often without you being aware of it. With this worry you can never really be happy, because happiness is when you feel at ease, attuned to your surroundings and not constantly irritated by doubts, fears, guilts, and uncertainties. This fundamental source of unhappiness is doubt and fear about the nature of the universe, what it is supposed to mean, and how we are supposed to behave toward it. Does it have a Creator and, if so, what and where is he, she, or it? These questions are at the back of everyone's mind, and if you are not reconciled to them you are never free of worry.

The science that is meant to cope with such worries by providing a reasonable account of the universe is properly called cosmology, but it bears little relation to what is practiced under that name today. Cosmos means the entire world system and everything in it, including ourselves and our thoughts about the cosmos. Modern cosmology does not pretend to describe the universe other than through astronomy and phys-

200

ics. The images it provides are obscure and fluctuating but generally of an alien universe with menacing black holes, mystifying super-strings, and other mathematically contrived phantasms. These are not images to live by, to comfort the old, to enliven children's patter. Surely, if our cosmologists had any idea what they were supposed to be doing, they could do better than that.

The ancients certainly did it better. Before modern science cosmologists everywhere understood that a world image has a formative effect on the minds of individuals and the societies they constitute. They knew that the cosmos is reflexive and that any image we project upon it will be returned to us again in the form of our life experience. They therefore looked for the most satisfactory cosmology, the picture of that world that accords with the known facts and with the structure of the human mind. They also knew that people and societies do better if they are centred upon the mystery of truth rather than self-centred, so they taught that God made the world as an imitation of Paradise. Their creative God was not adaptable to cults or beliefs, but combined all opposites and therefore had no positive attributes at all. According to the traditional cosmogony, as taught in the ancient and classical mystery schools, God took his compass, centred it upon a fixed point representing eternal law, and described the ever-spinning circle of the cosmos, beyond which there is nothing—or just more of the same. For reasons known to cosmologists and easily imparted to the simplest mind, he measured the circle's radius as the number 5,040 or the product of the numbers 1 to 7, or the number of miles between the centre of the earth and the centre of the tangent moon.

It is not to mystify that I mention this detail, but to indicate that there really is an ideal, scientific cosmology, firmly based on mathematical facts, unique and unchanging. Plato referred to it in a guarded way throughout his constitutional works. Those who learn it, he said, bring happiness to themselves and their friends. It comes, he added, through revelation. These present times are times of revelation. Obvious truths, long obscured by generations of materialistic education, are re-surfacing in minds, and the perennial cosmology will inevitably return to influence. You may not care to study it, said Plato, and in that case the best alternative is simple faith in God, because things are far better taken care of than we can possibly imagine. So there really is nothing to stop anyone being happy.

PART VII

Modern Madness

73

Jews, Christians, and the Heavenly Jerusalem

June 2000

*T*wo recent events have loosened tongues on subjects, which the media have hitherto avoided. One of them is the Pope's visit to the Holy Land, where he apologised to Jewry for the insults and injuries it has received from the Church, and the other is David Irving's controversial lawsuit. Irving lost his case but achieved possibly his main object, by stimulating open discussion of the historical rancour between Jews and Christians. I was pleased by these outbursts of candour, because they dragged these subjects up from the underworld of myth and rumour where they had long festered and exposed them to the light of rational discussion.

Holocaust studies are not in my line of business, but if Irving or anyone else wants to pursue them, good luck and free speech to him. My own interest is in the reconciliation of Jews and Christians. It is not just my ideal but part of our cultural heritage. The traditions of the British Church begin with Jewish missionaries from the Holy Land, and early chronicles refer to the British people as "God's true Israelites." These traditions were revived by the antiquarian William Stukeley in the eighteenth century. He identified the druidic temple at Avebury as a monument to true religious principles, still upheld by Jews and

Anglicans, and he foresaw that the free, happy situation of Jewish people in Britain would lead to "what many learned men have thought;
that here was to be opened the glory of Christ's kingdom on earth."
His follower William Blake reiterated our national prophecy, that here
in England will first be apparent that symbol of divine order restored to
earth, the heavenly Jerusalem.

Throughout most of the nineteenth century the most popular
and prestigious charity organisation in London was the Society for
Promoting Christianity among the Jews. Its noble patrons included
members of the royal family, and its president for many years was that
prince of do-gooders, the Earl of Shaftesbury—the Lord Longford of
his age. The Society's missionaries were sent to Jewish communities
all over the world, the idea being that, when the Jews were made into
Protestants and resettled in the Holy Land, they would breed the next
Messiah, and the world thereafter would be divinely ruled. Shaftesbury
persuaded the Prime Minister, his stepfather-in-law Palmerston, that
this scheme would both save the world and be to the advantage of the
British Empire.

For all its wealth and idealism, the Society for converting the Jews
was a complete flop. Hardly any Jews were converted by it, and when
they regained the Holy Land they were still Jews, not Protestants. You
cannot fairly blame them for taking advantage of a British obsession
which happened to work in their favour, but behind that obsession was
a glorious vision of the heavenly Jerusalem on earth. And for those who
want peace in the Holy Land and love between religions, the realisation
of that vision is far more useful than studies in anti-Semitism and the
cherishing of past grievances.

The Jews today are as confused as the rest of us, torn between religious and secular demands, rejecting the onus of Biblical prophecies
yet still in awe of them. Their innate or nurtured feeling that every
man's hand is against them fosters a corresponding reality. It grieves me
on visits to Jerusalem to see how traditional Catholic anti-Semitism is
matched by Jewish hatred for every feature of Christianity, including

their own man who preached universal love. Blind reactions are here at work, irrational and demonic. But on the other hand is reason, the light of which reveals that Jews and Christians are linked together by history and providence, and that nothing but prejudice and inherited rancour prevents them from living together on the normal, family level, which is the level of love. That is why the subject of traditional science and the heavenly Jerusalem is so much more interesting than Holocaust studies.

What has happened to time? Why is there now so little of it compared to the amount there used to be?

74

The Temple at Jerusalem

April 1994

Staying last month in the Jewish quarter of old Jerusalem, I could not help noticing the Muslims hurling rocks from the precinct of their mosque upon the Jews who were trying to stuff prayer papers in the Western Wall. Nor could I avoid seeing the unhelpful Holocaust Museum. Resentment, self-pity, fear, and hatred need no further encouragement in the land of Israel.

My purpose there was to confer with fellow idealists in the Academy of Jerusalem about the prophecies connected with the Holy City and their relevance to the present state of things in the Middle East. To the three "Abrahamic" religions—Jewish, Christian, and Muslim—Jerusalem is uniquely precious.

Simple congregations throughout the world sing of Zion as their spiritual home, for it is not just a material city but also, and above all, a symbol of that ideal "city," meaning the complete, divinely proportioned pattern of the universe, which at certain times is revealed again to needful humanity. Within it are to be reassembled all the twelve tribes of Israel, ten of which are now lost among the "nations of the world" implying a corresponding reconciliation between the allegorically numbered twelve races of mankind. To St. John in Revelation it was a sparkling, multicoloured, twelve-faceted vision, a state of perfect order and understanding. He not only saw it, he measured it, thus indicating that the heavenly Jerusalem is not just a dream but an ideal pattern that can actually be established upon earth.

Recent discoveries in Jerusalem are so remarkable and exciting that one can plausibly see revelation at work. First, Dr. Asher Kaufmann, physicist and learned rabbi, a native of Scotland, discovered the precise former site of the Temple, and his plan showed that the sacred rock once enclosed within the Holy of Holies was not the outcrop beneath the Islamic dome of the Rock, but another, due west of the Golden Gate. A still greater realisation followed: that the rock, the gate, the Temple axis, and also the rock of Golgotha, the central pivot of Christendom, stand together on one alignment, which, extended eastward, continues to the Mount of Olives.

On that straight, mystical pathway Jesus entered the city, and it is the traditional route by which the Messiah, the Mahdi, and the souls of the dead will make their way into Jerusalem. Further investigation shows that the ancient streets and monuments form a unified pattern over the city, which is the ground plan of Solomon's Temple but on a larger scale, six times greater than the original.

So Jerusalem is all one great temple. It is indeed that "house of prayer for all people," which Isaiah (56:7) prophesied as the future manifestation of the Temple. This only needs to be recognised, not created, for you can see as you walk its narrow alleys that the city actually is a universal temple, with people going about their various businesses, religious or secular, as if in a sanctuary.

Grave Jews in archaic costumes pass securely among the Arab traders who, speaking all languages, offer religious merchandise to pilgrim parties from every corner of the earth. The Jews say they are commanded by God to rebuild their Temple and renew the sacrifices in it; there are fanatics who want to prepare the ground by blowing up the Islamic dome. Such literalism is unnecessary, for the temple is already there, fully functioning, and it is not for any one sect or religion, but as the Prophet foretold, "for all people."

75
Two Dogs and a Bone

September 2000

When there is only one bone and two dogs are fighting over it, there is no room for compromise. That is a truth known to every village idiot, but it did not register with Mr. Clinton when he thought he could fiddle a deal between Jews and Muslims over Jerusalem. In a dog & bone situation you either let them fight it out or you confiscate the bone. The first option would be a disaster if applied to Jerusalem, whereas the second is not only possible but the ideal, natural, inevitable solution, which is also in accordance with prophecy. By confiscating the bone I mean raising Jerusalem—the holy, old city part of it—above the reach of politicians, re-consecrating it to its proper owner, the Almighty, and designating it a World Temple site under UN protection.

That would merely be recognizing the obvious fact of the matter—that old Jerusalem really is a temple and actually functions as one. A unique feature of this temple is that it is not exclusive to one faith but serves all three of the religions fathered by Abraham—Jewish, Christian, and Muslim. Each has some of its holiest shrines in old Jerusalem. Pilgrims from all continents assemble there and return home edified. The three religions do not much like each other, but that does not prevent them from sharing the old city as one temple.

It is the same situation in the Church of the Holy Sepulchre, the holiest place in Christendom, where the various churches who share the building, Eastern and Western, Catholic, Orthodox, and Coptic, are so quarrelsome amongst themselves that their keys are held by a hereditary Muslim doorkeeper. That is the status quo rather than the ideal situation, but it is stable enough to provide the basis for the next stage in Jerusalem's prophetic destiny—its recognition as (in the words of Isaiah 56:7) the temple "for all people." Jeremiah and other prophets insist that the temple, which is Jerusalem, shall be the sanctuary for every type and nation of humanity. This is not a reference to the distant future but to an actual, present reality, which is now in the process of being revealed.

At about the same time the Camp David talks about Jerusalem were broken off, my book *The Temple at Jerusalem: A Revelation* was launched at a party in Glastonbury, that curious little town in Somerset whose history and prophecies echo those of Jerusalem. The ruins of its Abbey occupy the site of our first Christian oratory where, in earlier times, teams of Druid choristers maintained a perpetual chant in harmony with the seasons and cycles. One day, says the prophecy, the sacred tradition will be restored there, bringing with it the state of divine order and happiness that is symbolised by the Holy Grail. It so happened that at the launch party Sir Cliff Richard was singing to thousands of Christians on the very site of the old perpetual choir within the Abbey. His distant voice was enchanting, and I had the pleasant feeling of prophecies approaching their fulfillment. I keep feeling this, and I know from personal experience and that of others that we are living in a time of revelation. But revelation of what? The short answer is that it is the revelation of a pre-existent, all-inclusive canon of number and harmony. Why is that important? Because it provides us with a true standard whereby to order ourselves and our societies, and because anyone who studies it is drawn toward the conclusion that the universe to which we are central is a divine creation. That is the traditional conclusion reached by learned people in all ages and recommended by them on two grounds: first because it is as near to the truth of things as our minds can grasp, and second because it comes naturally to our sense and leads the minds toward peace and happiness. That is the basic meaning of the revelation of Jerusalem the Temple.

76
God's Flower Garden

September 1992

*D*uring the Olympic Games, Christopher Booker in his *Sunday Telegraph* column observed that the eight finalists in the 100 metres (won by our own Linford Christie) were all "of West African descent." He further observed that East African runners dominated the middle- and long-distance events. Having broached this interesting subject he then became embarrassed and dropped it, muttering that no one could pursue it "for fear of being condemned as politically incorrect."

I was surprised that so senior a writer should be inhibited in his ruminations by such a trivial modern fad. It would be a blow for us generalisation-mongers to be deprived of our half-baked maunderings about the various characteristics of all nations. We do, however, seem to be threatened, and the danger comes from the current pseudo-orthodoxy, which upholds the brotherhood of man not by virtue of the fact that we are all God's people with the same immortal souls, but by the presumption that we are mere human units, identical and interchangeable. With this low view comes the absurd fantasy of a one-world culture, which means, in fact, no culture at all.

With it also comes the type of embarrassment suffered by Booker. I heard another example of this in a radio interview with an American sports coach. Asked to comment on the fact that almost all his star pupils were, like him, black, he grew uneasy and implied that it was a sort of coincidence. "I know that one day I'll find the great white sprinter," he said prayerfully. It was as if he found something shameful in the athletic prowess of black people. The same attitude is evident in the need to explain why so many black boxers are world champions. The reason, one is often told, is that they come from poor, disadvantaged families and see no other outlet for their ambitions. This sort of reasoning sadly degrades our pugilistic heroes.

Talking the other day with a friend "of West African descent" who works for the Race Relations Board, I remarked that her activities seemed largely to consist of seeking out grievances and giving them a good airing. Could she not, I wondered, find a more idealistic basis for racial harmony. Sensing my drift she told me about an old-fashioned book she had found in a library, the authoress of which compared the different races of mankind to the variety of flowers in God's herbaceous border. My friend said that she found this distasteful and patronizing and had recommended that the book be "de-shelved."

I looked up the lady's book and enjoyed it, particularly her emphasis on the beauty of hybrids. Her perception was similar to Plato's likening of the world to a dodecahedron made up of twelve differently coloured, pentagonal pieces of material. By that image he represented the traditional, orthodox belief that the twelve tribes of humanity, each placed under a different sign and with the corresponding tone, style, colour, temperament, and so on, form an ideal unity. Each tribe contributes its note to a twelve-part diatonic symphony in praise of the Creator. This means that we are not just components in a chaotic rabble, but that each of us adds a unique and necessary voice to the local, national, racial, and universal chorus. I could go on about this forever, but the point I want to hammer home is that every race, tribe, family, and human being has a particular aptitude and mode of praise, and this should not give rise to apologies but to joyful thanks for whatever gifts we have been allowed to bring toward the full expression of our common humanity.

77

A Multicultural Dream

June 2001

*A*rriving back at Waterloo from abroad, I rushed to buy the newspapers to see what was being chattered about and found them all playing the race game. A Tory MP had compared the British people to a glass of whisky which, when diluted with water, begins to look and taste different. By this he meant that our native white population has been so watered down by immigrants of different races and cultures that we are not the same people we were fifty years ago. That is indeed true but it is so obvious that it has become a truism, and refined people would never be so boring as to mention it. This blundering MP was not refined. He was, as critics soon reminded him, a provincial lout so ignorant of good manners and locution that in uttering his truism he seemed to be "playing the race card."

That is the wickedest card in the pack. In the political game it means pandering to ignorant voters within the majority group by inflaming their hates and fears of foreigners in their midst. The Nazis, of course, played it and came to power through it, so we are highly aware of its dangers and vigilant about it. No serious British politician in the whole of my postwar lifetime has ever blatantly played the race card. Enoch Powell was accused of it, but his oratory was cerebral, not rabble-rousing. Sir Oswald Mosley tried it but made a fool of himself, and none of the skinhead-fascist movements has ever attracted votes. The gradual colonisation of urban Britain by Asians, Africans, Turks, and all sorts of others has proceeded more or less peacefully with no active opposition from us natives or from our leaders. There has been no race card. We have just accepted the process. So what now?

There are two practical ways in which a still-dominant indigenous culture can come to terms with others that settle upon its territory. (The option of driving them out is, as the Red Indians soon recognised, not on.) One, as practiced by the colonial French, is to educate them in the native tradition, so that every child knows about Stonehenge, Julius Caesar, 1066, Henry VIII's wives, Shakespeare, Sherlock Holmes, and all that is indispensable for British crossword puzzles. That is chauvinistic alright, but it is still an option. The second way is to allow the various ethnic or religious groups to take over their own towns or parts of town, just as they do in New York, and to enact their own by-laws there—subject to the paramount law of the land.

I am very much in favour of this second way. It would restore to Britain the local diversity that was its glory in the days of its high culture. In those days every village had its own dances and music, every district its own peculiar laws and customs. Government was by true democracy—not the simulacrum of today. Each community elected by popular vote its own councilors, and they among themselves chose representatives for higher court . . . and so on up to the national assembly that elected the prime ruler. The advantage of this system is that everyone at every level votes for someone they actually know and respect. Applied to modern Britain it would have the gratifying result of allowing the minority communities to run their own affairs on the local level while ensuring that the majority retained overall control. Talented members of minorities could make their way to the highest positions— just as Disraeli did.

Like most native Britons, I would never have voted for "multiculturalism" if given the chance. But now that it is here I accept it as a product of God's will and see it as a divinely given opportunity for this country to regain its former condition as a land of many different tribes and peoples, where the highways are sacred and everyone can travel unmolested, but everywhere you go people are different—and you have to get on with them.

78
The New Crusaders

March 1993

There was a huge article in *The Guardian* the other day about an unloveable-sounding minx who writes prolifically in various organs of the gutter press. A headline announced that she hates Arabs and loves Stalin. I wondered how far she would have got if she had decided to hate Jews and love Hitler. The answer, of course, is that she would have got nowhere. It is illegal in Western Europe to express such opinions, and if anyone was so foolish as to print them the publications would be seized by the police.

I was amazed from the very beginning of the Salman Rushdie affair to hear that so many educated men and women were ranting on about the absolute right to free speech when they must have known that such a thing has never existed. One's rights in that matter amount to no more or less than what one can get away with. After all, would you exercise your presumed right to insult Mike Tyson to his face? The fact is that if you poke a stick into a hornets' nest they will rise up and sting you, no matter that you and your friends have proclaimed the right to free poking.

At a press conference held by Mr. Pinter and other bigwigs of the Rushdie Defence Committee, I became so intoxicated by the clouds of cant that I asked the great writers whether they would be so fervent about free speech if a large and previously respectable publisher issued a new edition of *The Protocols of the Elders of Zion,* the notoriously fraudulent exposure of a Zionist plot to subvert civilisation and take over the world. This powerfully written book has been the cause of far more deaths and misery than Rushdie's *Satanic Verses*—it would be murderously irresponsible to renew its influence. The Committee replied pleasantly that it was opposed to all prejudices from any direction—a good answer, although not exactly to my question.

Poor Rushdie is in a pitiful plight, and I am naturally among those who wish to protect him from the appalling consequences of his folly. Unfortunately, his leading defenders include those who encouraged and praised his blasphemies, using him for their own ends to promote their own narrow, secular, anti-religious worldview. By urging defiance, rather than allowing him to apologise and seek forgiveness, they have set him up to be a sacrifice to their own obsessions.

Apart from the merciless, ungodly death threat, the most alarming aspect of the Rushdie affair was the crude anti-Islamic abuse that emanated from English literature. The Muslims, we were told by popular novelists everywhere, are illiberal, fanatical, barbaric, cruel to women, and stuck in the Dark Ages. The Race Relations Act does not apply to religions or cultures, so such prejudices can lawfully be aired as substitutes for others that cannot. Yet, whatever the law says, stirring up hatred is a wicked thing to do. Do we really need the new Crusade that so many powerful voices and institutions seem to be fostering among us? Even if Brother Islam is as dreadful as they say—and no doubt among his millions there are just as many turbid fanatics as can be found in Jewry and Christendom—it is surely best to live with him in peace and friendship rather than go poking into that hornets' nest.

79
The Crusade Against Islam

July 1995

"The Flying Inn" is a story by St. G. K. Chesterton, set in the future when the Muslims take over England. The first thing they do is close down all the pubs. Yet they cannot stop the Flying Inn. Quaintly thatched and ingle-nooked, complete with busty barmaid, it descends every evening upon some English village and is off again by morning before the Muslim police can catch it.

It was a good story in its time, but it is hardly suitable for readers today. The modern mood is too fanatical to comprehend its subtle mysticism. Chesterton was no crusader against Islam but a traditionalist and defender of true orthodoxy. Had he been born in a Muslim country he would probably have written a story about a flying harem resisting the efforts of Christian intruders to impose monogamy.

Ever since the atrocities of the Reformation, which broke the religious enchantment of old England, our world has grown progressively more chaotic and uneasy. It must have been delightful at first, at the beginning of the seventeenth century, when free thinking became possible and the inspiring prospect arose of an ideal, rationally constituted commonwealth under the guidance of science. It was a lovely dream but with one fundamental and fatal flaw. The dreamers attributed to science the qualities of knowledge and wisdom, which properly belong to religion.

God is always one and the same, whereas science is an endless diversity, a cacophony of theories and opinions, never stable or self-consistent and quite incapable of deciding on the nature of things or of providing us with models and standards to live by. It has claimed to provide those things, but the failure of communism has proved most clearly its inability to do so. Scientists like to play God, but they will never find a substitute for the real thing.

Against the spread of secularism, usury, and the evils of materialism throughout the world there is only one formidable source of opposition—the religious law of Islam. That is the reason for the hateful anti-Muslim sentiments that are now being stirred up in us.

It is easy enough to find fault with these people. Like all foreigners they have some obnoxious customs, and they should perhaps have been more appreciative of Rushdie's witty insults to their religion. Yet surely we should admire and be grateful to them for standing up to us, for resisting the fads of modernism and holding firm to their conceptions of the divine order on earth. In trying to imitate God's law they inevitably make mistakes, but these they will doubtless correct in their own good time—and all the sooner if we Western know-it-alls stop shouting orders at them. I do not know much about the Muslim world, but see it in normal times as comparable to pre-Reformation England, simple, peaceful, and orderly under the spell of Allah.

If you are secure in yourself and dwell in a state of love rather than fear, you feel no need for enemies. Our secular world is not secure, so it does need an enemy, and Islam has been appointed to that role. Abusing people on grounds of their race is against the law, but active prejudice against the Muslim culture and religion is fomented today on all levels with impunity. Chesterton's light fantasy about a Muslim takeover has been blown up into a monstrous phobia. I should hate to be thought a traitor, but patriotism ranks far below the first Commandment, and even the Queen could not persuade me to join our nation's crusade on behalf of liberal atheism. Apart from the principle of the thing, those Mohammedans are holy terrors when you stir them up.

80
The Matter of Ireland

March 1992

According to Geoffrey Wheatcroft in *The Sunday Telegraph,* the problem of Ireland is insoluble. That is only true within the conventions of modern thinking. The history of Ireland shows that the same problem as today, of one island containing different peoples, has always existed and there has always been the same ideal solution to it.

Ancient Ireland was divided into four provinces: Ulster (N), Munster (S), Leinster (E) and Connacht (W). Each province had a king and managed its affairs at a seasonal meeting, which was imitated by lesser assemblies for each region and clan.

On the day of the national festival the four provincial chiefs, each with two lesser kings and a hierarchically ordered retinue, formed a ceremonial group around the High King in Meath (Middle), regarded as the fifth province, situated between the other four at the centre of the island.

The authority of the High King was mystical and symbolic. At his installation he was ritually married to the female spirit of Ireland, and he represented the unity of the country. His duties were mainly cultural, to uphold standards of music, poetry, and the arts and to maintain established customs. As chairman to the council of twelve provincial leaders, he ratified their agreements and sanctioned laws and initiatives on behalf of the nation, but it was not his business to interfere directly in the governing of tribes and regions.

This was the traditional model of society known in all the Celtic realms, in Scandinavia, throughout Greece, in Africa and the East and, at different times, worldwide. Based on a traditional cosmology and a science of statecraft now temporarily forgotten, it was supposed to allow the greatest possible amount of personal and local independence within a federal structure that was supported largely by the power of sanctified custom, myth, and music.

In affirming that this ideal model, diluted, is the inevitable and practical means of bringing about the happiness of Ireland—and many other afflicted countries—one is merely being orthodox and unoriginal.

Nothing in this proposal is new-fangled or invented, for the restoration of Ireland's High King is only the restoration of normality.

All this was seen ten years ago by Constantine FitzGibbon, who imagined a federation of the four historic provinces in which "each would elect its own parliament and have its own police force and complete control of its own internal affairs." His choice for the national capital was Armagh where reside both the Roman Catholic and the Church of Ireland primate.

The practical solution to the problem of Ireland is also the ideal solution. Unfortunately, due to deep-rooted errors in modern education, the ideal and the real are commonly regarded as different and irreconcilable. Yet, as Plato taught, unless you clarify and actively pursue the ideal you will never get anywhere.

Politicians tinker around with low-level plots and pacts which irritate all parties, but were they to raise their eyes and contemplate the ideal, they could not only please everybody but spread lasting delight over the whole country.

As to who should be the High King or High Queen (subject to adjustments of the mating ritual at the coronation) of Ireland, that is none of my business. Since his or her duties consist mainly of patronizing the national and cultural institutions and receiving foreign dignitaries, any educated and well-mannered old boy or old girl would do—for the time being. Soon, of course, under the influence of idealism, higher perceptions will prevail and Ireland will once more be ruled by philosopher kings and sagely administered by bards and scholars. Is this not exactly what everyone wants?

What has happened
to time? Why is there now so little of it
compared to the amount there used to be?
properly into those

81
The Burning of a Prophet
June 1993

I was horrified to read in the papers about the death of poor David Koresh. He and almost the whole of his Bible-reading class, about ninety people in all, were burnt to death in the hostel he was running at Waco, Texas, during a fracas with the local Bureau of Alcohol, Tobacco, and Firearms. Like most prophets he had his paranoid side and would not let them in until they assaulted him with tanks, one of which is said to have knocked over a table with an oil lamp on it—which is easily done when you are driving a tank through a living room—and the whole place went up in flames. Poor David is thought to have shot himself rather than go through the agony of burning. He was only thirty-three, far too young for martyrdom.

The tragedy reminded me of another, which happened earlier, when members of a cult barricaded themselves against the authorities, shot at them from their fortress and, before their leader could be arrested, committed mass suicide. The authorities on that occasion were Roman, and the cultists who defied them were the Zealots of Masada, Israel, during the first century AD. Like the Waco group they read their Bible and bore witness against the materialism of their age. Both groups died for their faith, so both are properly called martyrs.

My connection with David was that we were both admirers of a previous Prophet Koresh, originally called Dr. Cyrus Teed of Chicago, who in 1885 led his followers to Florida where they formed an ideal community. They had a strange creed, believing that the world was a hollow sphere with the sun at its centre and that we live on its inner surface. This implies that the earth's surface is concave and not, as most people believe, convex. Koresh was scientific and he devised an instrument, the Rectilineator, to test his theory. It projected a dead straight line, starting a few feet above and parallel to a stretch of flat, sandy beach. After a few miles the line met the surface of the earth, thus establishing that the world we inhabit is, in fact, concave. Confirmed in their faith, the Koreshans lived happily and harmlessly in their seaside paradise until their leader was murdered by the local sheriff.

One result of the Rectilineator experiment was that it showed how scientific methods can be used to prove whatever theory or notion you apply them to, and thus it helped to eradicate my respect for empiricism. The exemplary life of Koresh made a chapter in my book *Eccentric Lives*. David, however, wanted to emulate him. He adopted the name and doctrines of Koresh and, from what I heard, this community at Waco began as successfully as the earlier Floridian venture. No one really wants to die for his beliefs, and I am sure David did not enjoy the martyrdom that was forced upon him, even though he must have known what was coming. His speciality, and the subject of his most inspirational sermons, was the Book of Revelation, particularly the story of Babylon. That rich, predatory city, which he equated with modern America, devoured its prophets and was then itself consumed by a holocaust. All of us who enjoy paranoid insights are attracted by this story, but as David's example shows, it is fatal to allow one's mind to become modeled upon it. If you do so it will all come true.

Dying for one's beliefs is utterly fanatical, but one cannot help sympathizing with Babylon's victims, from the heroes of Masada to the young Koreshans of Waco. Many of David's followers were British, but I do not suppose that our Man in America will have much to say about that. After all, they were merely "cultists."

82
Bringing Light to Europe

December 1996

*D*iana Mosley let the cat out of the bag with her letter in *The Sunday Telegraph* (6 October), cheering on the movement for European unity and saying it was just what her late husband, Sir Oswald, had worked for. So that explains it. These born-again fascists are popping up everywhere. It is not that I am prejudiced against Mosley. Like poor Blunt and the other so-called traitors, he wanted the best for his own country, and there was something heroic as well as ridiculous about him. I used to read a sort of literary magazine he put out, *The European,* from which I learnt that the destiny of Europe was to be united in a single white-man's state with Africa as its "bread-basket."

The African bread-basket is no longer available and has been replaced by Eastern Europe. Apart from that and the fact that its rulers will be German rather than British, the proposed European Union is indeed similar to the Mosley model. This has given me something positive to say in conversations with Eurofanatics. These people used to stun me with their dreary talk about economic necessity, but now I can help them on to a higher level, reminding them of the glorious vision of One Europe that Mosley inherited from Hitler. After a few moments of this talk the Eurofiends are wishing I would take my enthusiasm elsewhere. I wonder if Lady Mosley really thought she was helping the EC by resurrecting Sir Oswald as its founder.

In the debate over Europe the side that must certainly be in the right are the heretics who stand nobly by our sovereign and sovereignty. The reason they have to be right is that their opponents, who recommend union with the continent, are supported by the accredited experts both in politics and economics, and it is a well-observed phenomenon that the official theorists in every field turn out always to be wrong—not just slightly and sometimes wrong—but totally and invariably. I have long wondered why this should be so and now have an inkling of the reason, but cannot briefly share it.

The natural relationship between these islands and the continent is not too difficult to see; it is illustrated throughout our history. In the European imagination Britain is always pictured as a land apart, a land of mystery and magic, holy, haunted, and weirdly inhabited. Every summer the mystical youth of Europe are drawn to this country by the common belief that ghosts and phantoms, ancient sanctuaries, romantic legends, UFOs, crop circles, and the like can best be studied and discussed here. This is a very old tradition. In pagan times the continental nobles used to send their children on courses of initiation to the mystical druid colleges of Britain, and in the sixth century, when Europe lay groaning under the burden of Roman materialism, those same colleges, reformed into Christian monasteries, sent forth a wave of Celtic and Anglo-Saxon missionaries to remind their benighted neighbours about the existence of angels.

The Europeans have terribly erratic memories. They have forgotten about angels once again, and their present occupation is patching together a would-be "superstate," partly through fear of the rest of the world and partly through desire to dominate it. Like all such imitations of Great Babylon, this Eurostructure will inevitably fall, bringing down with it our economic system and the fabric of civilised living. That does not worry me anymore. I have just discovered and am trying to adopt the way of life called "Quietism." It is very suitable for older people. A Quietist gives up all hopes, fears, and ambitions, expects no special favours from heaven and gratefully accepts whatever God or fate has in store for him. So they can do what they like about Europe. We Quietists are barred from interfering in such matters, and even if Goldsmith holds his referendum we shall leave the outcome to divine will and the votes of other people.

83
The Closed Loop

July 1993

A youth lounging in my street showed me his can of Belgian lager. Above the brand name was the legend, "Anno 1366." "Do you believe that?" he asked. Not wanting to encourage cynicism I merely said it was a bold claim. They may, I suppose, have drunk that filthy lager in the fourteenth century, but it seems unlikely, and there was no such country as Belgium before 1830.

Years ago when I watched television I was amazed every evening by the literally incredible claims of the advertisers: brewers especially. I wondered how they managed to get away with it, and one day, having nothing better to do, thought it would be interesting to find out. The most preposterous advertisement at that time was by the makers of a canned lager called "Long Life." It was, they kept repeating, "the very first beer brewed specially to drink at home."

This was a ridiculous thing to say. Ever since Druid times, and well into the eighteenth century, every farmer and many cottagers brewed their own beer and drank it at home. The Long Life people should have known that, and to spare them the embarrassment of parading their ignorance any further I wrote them a kind letter pointing out the mistake. This was unanswered, so I did what you are supposed to do in these cases, and complained to the Independent Broadcasting Authority.

It was their business to check every claim made by advertisers on television and to make sure they were true.

My letter was answered, very audaciously, by their Mr. Jack Smith. The Long Life claim, he said, was justified because they were the first people in Britain to sell beer in cans rather than bottles. That, of course, was quite a different matter, and I wrote back to say so. Mr. Smith replied that there was only a "fine distinction" between beer made for drinking at home and beer brewed for cans. The Long Life claim had been running for many years, and though it must at one time have been tried, tested, and officially approved, the original documentation was found to be "no longer available."

This blatant fobbing-off sharpened my interest and I sent Jack Smith some other cases of false or misleading advertising. One was for a kind of white paint whose special virtue, according to its makers, lay in it being made up of "molecules that lock together." These molecules were shown on the screen as little spheres, which do not interlock, so either the image or the statement must have been wrong. Poor Jack (we had grown quite friendly) did his good-natured best, but it was obvious that the whole testing process was a farce. So I asked him how and to what higher authority I could appeal against his prevarications. You could, he amusingly replied, write to the Advertising Authority or to the Home Secretary, but in either case the letter would be referred back to him to deal with. The whole thing was a closed loop.

Since then I have wasted no more time complaining. These loops are everywhere, in business, politics, and all professions, and I now appreciate the loyalty that makes people defend their own kind against outsiders. Hunters talk about controlling vermin, but actually they conserve the animals they chase, and a similar bond exists between advertisers and those who are supposed to regulate them. It is quite natural and as it should be. Unless you are a crusading moralist you can only accept it as one of the principles by which the Great Inscrutable makes the world go round.

84
Evil Conspiracies

April 1996

*W*hen I was at school the history master warned us about conspiracy theories. These, he said, are adopted by weak-minded people who cannot accept that the stupid, unjust way of the world is a result of normal human confusion, and believe that a sinister group of plotters must be behind it all.

This was the first time I had heard of conspiracy theory, and the master's warning had the natural effect of attracting me to it. Previously I had read that the non-existence of witches was a rumour put around for their own security by witches themselves, and this dubious information led me to suspect that our teacher was up to the same game. Why should he forbid us to seek out conspiracies unless he himself was involved in one?

Freed at last from the influence of academic opinions I went properly into the subject, beginning with the infamous *Protocols of the Learned Elders of Zion,* a tract that has been held largely responsible for the persecution and murder of Jews in modern Europe. Probably written by an anti-Bolshevik Russian monk, Nilus, who lifted its theme from an earlier fiction-writer, it purports to reveal the methods by which a ruling council in Jewry plans to dominate the world. Their idea is to confuse and corrupt the Gentiles, causing them to mock religion, turn against lawful rulers and lose faith in their own instincts and values, thus making them easy prey to the evil schemers.

The *Protocols* is an imaginary work but a very powerful one, because even when the Jewish elders are taken out of it, its central theme remains indestructible. Our history master was quite right to warn us about conspiracy theories, but he was wrong in implying that these only affect the weak-minded. Great Thinkers, scholars, theologians, not to mention politicians, have been convinced that there really is an organised, purposeful power of evil in the world. We liberals are not supposed to believe in Satan and evil powers, but we too are human, and I have never known a human mind that was entirely unsusceptible to these bugbears. Nilus's formula for a bestseller is as effective today as it has always been.

The *Protocols* are discredited, the commie threat has receded, and the international bankers are plainly just as confused as the rest of us, but conspiracy mania is a hydra with many heads, and when one is lopped off others appear, even more fantastical. Like everything else they follow fashion, and this season's mode is extra-terrestrial.

On recent trips to the USA, every other person that I have met, grave and senior though they be, has alerted me to the alien menace with details of abductions, infiltrators, and secret government bases where special agents are examining captured spacemen. This nonsense, I reply lightly, is part of a worldwide conspiracy against ordinary common sense.

But what I really want to say is that all conspiracy-mongers of all types are suffering from the same one thing: they have lost faith in God. The dominant image in their minds is the image of evil, and its name is Legion for it is many. You can spend your life chasing demons and exposing wickedness, but you will never achieve anything real because in the world of illusion there is nothing real to achieve. The only reality, the only thing worth pursuing, is not Legion but One.

My dear friends, I long to tell the conspiracy addicts, please don't worry too much about the machinations of the Adversary. Insofar as he exists he is a mere detail in the universe, and that is how he should be in your mind. Forget the Devil, make God your centre, and from the very moment of that decision you will live as sanely and happily as nature intends you to.

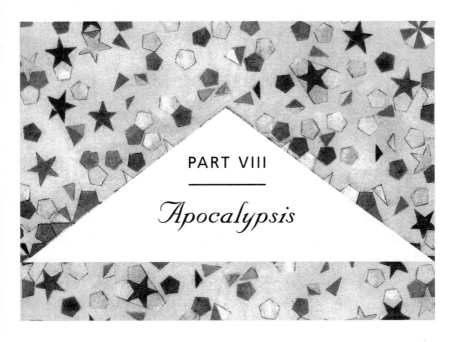

PART VIII

Apocalypsis

85

The Modern Illusion

February 1994

*W*herever and however you look at the world, you cannot help but notice that everything is in a state of crisis verging upon collapse. There is no mystery about the cause of this; it is because of our education. Throughout the modern period we have learnt to see the world in a certain limited way, as described by science, and to adapt our minds so that happiness and well-being are identified with material progress. Official policies and institutions are all based on that idea and are designed only to serve it. So there we are, all in the same boat and heading rapidly toward the rocks which surround us in every direction. I think it would be best to turn off the engine while we consider our position.

We are not really on a boat at all. It just seems like it because mentally we have been cast adrift. Our imaginations, which form the world we experience, have been loosed from their moorings, and that is why we feel so dangerously at sea. We have lost touch with our normal, traditional way of thinking and are obsessed by ugly illusions. How did this happen and what are we to do about it?

The most dreadful series of illusions came upon us in the nineteenth century. Great men, ape-like, often with large beards, roamed the earth proclaiming theories. Typically they had no interest in human nature and did not even believe in it, presuming that people could be improved, or at least rationalised, by order of state. Nor did they acknowledge the limits which nature imposes upon us. Man, they believed, was meant to conquer and subjugate nature, even to liquidate it. That was Marx's view. In his *Manifesto* he called for "Subjugation of nature's forces to man, machinery, application of chemistry to industry and agriculture," and so forth, culminating in "the clearing of whole continents for cultivation." No doubt, given the chance, he would have cleared Africa first. As it was, his disdain for nature and rural life enabled Stalin to liquidate the peasantry, and the final result of Marxian thinking is the thorough pollution of once-holy Russia by industrial and nuclear poisons. Mao in China continued the war for socialism against nature, killing even more people in the process and devastating large areas of his own countryside.

How could the spiritually intense Russians and the crafty, philosophical Chinese have fallen for such a callow, coarse illusion? Eventually, of course, they will find the way back to their own traditional cultures. It will be a hard process, but they are not the only people who have to undergo it. We have all been subjected to the same low type of illusion that Marx upheld. It is still the prevailing influence in science and education, in politics, economics, and general understanding of the world. Somehow we have to throw it off.

We shall have to talk further about this subject. The problem is clear enough, that we are in the grip of a certain worldview and cast of mind for which there are many adjectives—materialistic, rationalistic, atheistic, progressive, and so on—which is taking us straight to hell and destruction. It is a man-made thing so it will not last for very long, but the longer it continues the harder will be the path to sanity. So the question is how, as an ordinary, well-meaning individual, can one be most helpfully effective? We shall consider some options—Green Party, New Age consciousness, saving the whale, or just grabbing what you can while it lasts.

What has happened
to time? Why is there now so little of it
compared to the amount there used to be?

86

Chasing the Millennium

September 1994

O ne of the most influential books in my generation was Norman
Cohn's *The Pursuit of the Millennium,* about the recurrent feeling that the world is about to come to an end and how people react to
this. From early Christian to our own times prophets have foreseen the
imminent destruction of society, followed by revelations, and finally by
the establishment of a divine or ideal order of affairs upon earth.

Millennium fever often afflicts desperate people who feel that their
lives and cultures are threatened by implacable forces and see no way
out of the situation. One form of response, typical of many, was that
of the Midwest Indians. When their sanctuaries and hunting grounds
were seized by settlers they performed the Ghost Dance to bring back
the old times, wove themselves garments of invulnerability and took on
the US Army, who gunned them down. Their bodies were shoveled into
trenches, and towns such as Madison, Wisconsin, were built over them.

The reason I mention this subject is that for many years I have been
gripped by the feeling that the basis of our civilisation is so fragile and
artificial that the whole thing could collapse at any minute. It is a true
axiom that all man-made things—indeed, all material things—wither
and vanish, so the collapse is inevitable, but my mistake has been in
expecting it sooner rather than later. Many others have been misled in
the same direction.

William Cobbett gave a public dinner, with tables ranged down the high street of Farnham, to celebrate the failure of a local bank, believing that it marked the end for capitalist usury. For years I have been reading and half-believing books by learned authors proving that by 1960, '70, '90, or whenever, we would be bombed, starved, polluted, overcrowded, burnt, or flooded to death. Yet here we still are, eating, making money, enjoying the trivia of life, just as if everything was normal.

All the same I am still influenced by the millennial notion with its patter of destruction, revelation, and the appearance of a new order. Norman Cohn points out how disastrous this notion has often been, how conducive to madness and fanaticism. Psychologists are also against it for similar reasons. Even I recognise it as a form of mental obsession, like Marxism, which can colour your whole perception of life and thus become self-confirming. Yet I cannot see it as essentially evil, for it has inspired the greatest poetry and prophecy, and its constant reappearance in so many different forms shows that it is an inherent part of human nature. The millenarian idea, therefore, has a true function. It is our natural response to times like the present, of uncertainty and menace.

My own policy is to accept and mentally refine it, to study for example the dimensions of the Heavenly City of Revelation 21, and learn thereby to appreciate that traditional code of science and philosophy which, by the millennial process, will one day rise up again to overwhelm the mishmash of secular fads and theories that constitutes the accepted wisdom of today.

A well-known delusion which arises from millennial thinking is that you are one of an elect group, chosen to save or enlighten the world. My prophylactic against that is the example of the Prophet Judd, who arose in California about 1965. After a year's solitude and dope-smoking, he heard a voice bidding him to lead his followers to a certain high mountain where they would survive a cataclysm. "Why have I been chosen for this great task?" asked Judd, awestruck; and the voice replied, "Because you are so gullible."

87
The End Is Nigh-ish
February 1996

*T*he only reason I do not proclaim the imminent End of the World is that it has been proclaimed so often, over so many hundreds of years, that it seems right to be cautious.

Some people say that if you think the world is coming to an end you are merely thinking about your own death. There is surely something in that, but behind one's feelings of personal mortality lies the universal truth that all created things have but a limited period of existence and finally perish. Human institutions are particularly fragile. From great empires to great theories, everything we invent, establish, and regard as real lasts only for a short time. So it is quite safe to predict that the world-order we have built up will one day crumble. The only question is: when?

The when? question is unanswerable; many prophets of doom have made the mistake of setting a precise date and thereafter looking foolish. Kathleen Raine's mystical perception is that the Kali Yuga (the final age in the cycle) still has a long time to go.

The prophets often underestimate the ruthlessness with which a dominant system is prepared to defend itself, and one can see that there are many places and peoples in the world that have yet to be assimilated by the world economy. So there is still room for expansion, and that means that there is still some way to go—or so it seems. But the catastrophe theorists have shown that systems do not just gradually decline and fade away but change suddenly from order to chaos. As Ian Sommerville put it: every day the queue at the post office grows longer, until one day it is no longer a queue but a mob.

Prophesying the End is not a job for amateurs but should be left to those who have qualified themselves for it by studies in cyclical history. This subject has its own technical, alchemical language in which to describe the successive stages that every civilisation passed through, from foundation to destruction. Among its products are Plato's account of Atlantis and St. John's Fall of Babylon. Behind these is the same archetypal theme of a world-order symbolised by a city-state.

It was well founded, and as long as its rulers upheld the divine code of law, imparted to them at the beginning, the citizens had as much happiness as any society can provide. But in the course of time they grew lax, neglected their laws and customs, and lost respect for their elders. The city became an empire, exploited its neighbours and imported foreign luxuries to the ruin of its native economy. The divine, indivisible One that inspired its foundation gave way to the Many—the multiple illusions and appetites of Mammon. Corrupted by wealth, the citizens turned morose and quarrelsome. They declined politically from government by dedicated initiates through decent democracy to mob rule exercised by the most vicious and vulgar.

That situation has its inevitable product: a mighty, self-centred dictator. He is hailed at first because he promises to restore order and keep things going; but he is a type of Antichrist, and when he appears it is an infallible sign that the End is at hand. You can neither get rid of him nor divert him from the path to holocaust.

We have seen some fine specimens of dictators this century, but Hitler, Stalin, and the rest will seem tin-pot compared to the one, which, by all respectable criteria, we must fairly soon expect. He has not arisen yet, so it is probably right that the world still has some time to run. I cannot even see him coming—unless it is that man who makes computers—but my feeling is, the way things are going, that he will probably turn out to be a Chinaman.

88
What of the Future, My Friend?

September 1997

A well-known state in senility is when you start complaining that everything is going downhill or, as the old boys used to say, going to the dogs. If you keep saying that, everyone thinks you are an old bore, and they are probably right. But you could be right also. There are, after all, certain yardsticks by which you can distinguish between a healthy society and one that is going to the dogs. For example, in the sounds we produce there is a real and measurable difference between good conversation and mindless grunting, between music—properly so called—and random noise. The same goes for art, where it is obvious to any sane person that a well-made painting or sculpture is aesthetically superior to a pile of dead rats. I have not actually seen the rats, nor have I yet been to the current ICA exhibition of a plain, plumbed-in-lavatory. But I once saw the famous pickled sheep and found a melancholy sort of pleasure in the contortions of pious visitors trying to make sense of it.

In seeing a decline, or total collapse, of standards in art and music, the old bores are undoubtedly correct. And they are equally right in complaining about the level of popular culture and conduct. Many young people can hardly talk any more, let alone sing. To spare themselves embarrassment, they go to pubs where the noise is amplified so as to make speech impossible. The prophetic ex-goalkeeper David Icke suspects an evil conspiracy as the cause of modern chaos, but this insight makes him worried and unhappy and that is why I avoid that way of thinking. My own chosen attitude is total confusion. The world has changed so thoroughly that I hardly recognise it as the same place I grew up in. UFOs, spacemen, and crop circles had never been heard of in those days, and it was possible to meet any number of American ladies without hearing about their abduction experiences and extra-terrestrial brain implants. A solid US citizen told me this summer that he comes from the Pleiades and communicates with his ancestors there. He says there are millions like him and, from the number of weird types around these days, I can well believe it. The question I keep asking is this—granted that the world is going rapidly insane, is this a sign of the approaching Last Days, or is it a natural, inevitable stage in the working-out of God's Purpose?

It could, of course, be both. Nothing material or man-made lasts forever, and all our institutions of finance and technology are bound, sooner or later, to meet their Last Days. If God has a Purpose, the constant destruction of all human artifacts seems to be a necessary part of it. New Age mystics and those in touch with Pleiadeans say that we shall soon be moving, effortlessly, without undue suffering or upheaval, into a world dominated by Love rather than Fear, but that is so weak and unrealistic that I do not even try to believe in it. When the Last Days come—for a human life, an empire, an economics system, an academic theory, or a living planet—the end they bring is total, final, and often painful. One day there will be an almighty crash, compared to which the Fall of Babylon in Revelation was but a splash in the ocean. Death and destruction will be massive and widespread, but that is nothing to worry about. If you are a Quietist, you accept God's will unconditionally, expecting nothing in return for your devotion. That way you can never be disappointed. The reincarnationists threaten us with a long series of future existences, but I no more believe them than I believe the atheists who preach the mortality of the soul. A Quietist lives in a state of contented confusion. As to the future, I apply to it Mr. Major's wise words on the problem of Europe—best wait and see.

89

Millennial Prognostications

End of Year 1999

A game that is always popular, and especially now with the year 2000, is divining the future. It is a pleasant indulgence, and I was pleased to see a collection of predictions by various specialists in *Cam,* the Cambridge University magazine. The contributors are reasonable and moderate in the Cambridge tradition. They speak of problems and crises—of population growth, the extinctions of species, and the effects of global warming. The Dutch are advised to heighten their dykes and the Bangladeshis to learn how to swim. But for the most part the experts see things going on much as before, sometimes more efficiently. Against this consensus is Dame Margaret Anstee, a Newnham girl who became Under-Secretary of the United Nations. She worries about terrorists, drug traffickers, and local warlords, particularly when they acquire atomic weaponry. Her answer to these and other threats is a one-world, UN authority. That is an alarming prospect, but her good news is that it is unlikely. The only thing that could achieve world unity, she imagines, would be an invasion from outer space. The other experts do not encourage this fantasy. There is still no evidence of life, even microscopic, beyond earth, writes New Hall astronomer, Jacqueline Mitton, and the chances of finding intelligent life in space "aren't great." Over thirty years ago the Americans claimed to have landed on the moon, but that has never been repeated. Our present technology will allow space-stations to orbit the earth, but there is no prospect, outside the imagination of science-fiction writers, of exploration beyond the solar system. We are alone with our problems, and it is up to us Cambridge people to solve them.

As an old Trinity man, that strikes me as a sensible conclusion. But as an old mystic who has weighed up the evidence, I find that we are not actually alone. Throughout the whole of human experience, from tribal wanderings to every type of civilisation, we have been impelled to recognise other participators in our state of being—godly, ghostly, inspirational, daimonic, bringers of good luck or ill health—that constantly impinge upon our existence. I agree with the Cambridge experts in discounting extra-terrestrials, but my probings into the origin of culture incline me to accept Plato's statement, in the *Laws,* that the arts of civilisation have been imparted to us from time to time by the gods. This is echoed in myths universally. "There was a time," says Plato, "when the gods ruled directly, and there was a time when they had to leave." Before departing they chose certain people to succeed them and initiated them into the laws and principles behind divine governance. As long as these were maintained the Golden Age continued; but we humans are lazy, we neglect and lose our most valuable traditions, and gradually we decline through plutocracy and democracy into anarchy and confusion. That is when we cry out for help, and from somewhere that cry is answered.

The answer, when it comes, takes the form of a revelation. That does not mean a god or UFO descending, but something that enters minds just when it is needed. Basically it is a pattern or codification of number, and as you study it you realise that it is the pattern of creation and of the human mind. It has been the foundation pattern of civilisations from very ancient times, because it provides the blueprint for a justly ordered, long-lasting form of society. Among relics of this revelation in the past are the old units of measure, preserved in the monuments of all nations, which everywhere represent simple fractions of the earth's dimensions. Images of it include the city of heavenly order that St. John described in Revelation 21. My unasked-for but readily given contribution to Cambridge's prognostications is that this is a time of revelations. The future will be quite different from anything that the experts prophesy, because it will not be a development from the present but a complete break with it.

90

The Beast in Man

February 2000

*I*t is soothing to read things you agree with, but writings by people with different ideas from your own have a painful effect and one is inclined to avoid them. The natural result is that one's prejudices are constantly being confirmed. One of my prejudices is against Darwinism and the theories of an expanding universe and human progress that go with it. Thus I eschew the writings of Hawking, Dawkins, materialists, evolutionists, and all who give me pain. Instead I seek comfort and solace in works of true orthodoxy by authors who are not taken in by the farrago of rootless doctrines that constitutes the pseudo-orthodoxy of today.

Just before Christmas, however, on a visit to sunny Cyprus, I was confronted with a pile of books on the "selfish gene," the "demonic male," the "beast in man," and so on, and compelled to read them. This came about through a deal with my old college friend, George Tomaritis, a shell and fossil expert and proprietor of a natural history museum. He is a lawyer, so loves to argue, and his side of the argument is that God and religion are red herrings, distracting us from the scientific facts of our evolution from apes. But like many professed atheists and pessimists, George is not happy in that state of mind and would really like to be argued out of it. Our deal was that I should read some of his evolutionist books while he read a selection from my anti-Darwin collection.

I am not sure what effect my books had on George, but one of his made a strong impression on me. It had an off-putting title, *The Rise and Fall of the Third Chimpanzee,* and its author, Jared Diamond, is a cocky know-all with explanations for everything, from the origin of language to the reasons we drink, smoke, and copulate. But he does know his natural history, he writes well, and his book gave me a good shaking-up. We people are just a fancy kind of chimpanzee, he says, and chimps are cruel bastards, fighting and murdering their neighbours at every opportunity. Wherever we go about the earth, as hunters, traders, or colonisers, we massacre any natives and destroy the local wildlife. This is not just white man's mischief, it is how we all behave. The first Asian hunters who entered North America some 11,000 years ago quickly exterminated the big game throughout the entire continent. Then it was their turn to be hounded into near-extinction—by our colonial cousins. Diamond is a chronicler of holocausts, both animal and human, which grew in number and scale throughout the bloody twentieth century. Everyone knows what the Turks did to the Armenians and the Nazis to Jews and Gypsies, but the millions liquidated in those holocausts are outnumbered by the victims of more recent mass murders. And the mass exterminations of wildlife, large and small, animal and vegetable, is so speeding up that quite soon the only places we can meet chimpanzees will be in zoos.

Trying to be optimistic, Diamond thinks that we may save ourselves. There may be some universal agreement to curb human nature and perhaps even change it. Our government seems to be thinking that way, with its banning of manly sports and its encouragement of the feminine within us. That is the New Age agenda, and good luck to it. But human nature is not changeable. We will probably complete the trashing of our earth while fighting over what is left, and survivors will return to our natural state of tribal nomadism.

Why not? It has happened many times before. The geological record displays successive cataclysms followed by periods of regeneration when new species suddenly appear. The world will be made rich again, and our descendants will inherit a natural paradise. Then they will make the mistake of settling down, and the cycle will start again. If any readers can see a more likely outcome from the present situation, I should be glad to hear from them.

91

Old Boys,
New Agers, and
Sacred Order

August 1993

I love my contemporaries but some of them are infuriating. Aged sixty or more, they think of themselves as modern-minded, and this leads them into all kinds of awkwardness and error. They patronise modern art and architecture and some of them still pretend to like modern music and dancing. At a dear old friend's birthday party the other day the music (properly called "noise") was so loud and raucous that I could not hear a word of what the other dear old friends were saying and, even worse, they could not hear my nonsense. When I asked the host if the sound could not be turned down or, preferably, off, he gave a silly leer and said I was getting old-fashioned.

Some of these old boys have their minds fixed in the same pattern as when we were at school. They believe in the metric system, the theory of evolution, Freudian psychology, the inferiority of ancient and other races, the idea of progress, intellectual egoism, and other fads of our misguided youth, even the wearing of jeans. They do not understand that business about Maastricht, but it sounds modern so they are all in favour of it. Nor do they have the slightest notion of how computers

251

work, but they pretend they do, so they spend millions of pounds on dud equipment, placing their firms in the hands of callow computer operators who run everything downhill.

The generation which saw the coming of telephones, gramophones, motor cars, and so on, lived through more external changes than we have, but socially and mentally the world since the War has changed more radically than in any previous period. The threat of annihilation, beginning with the Bomb, has deepened with pollution, the death of species, the corruption of learning, and the universal collapse of cultures. No human mind can resolve these crises, so we fiddle around with petty politics and computer games, vaguely hoping that somehow we can at least save the whale. It is a sad prospect, quite different from the progressive future we were taught to expect.

In reaction to this, New Age thinking has arisen. Turning sharply away from everything learnt at school, people are healed by scents and crystals, communicate with dolphins and demons, consult oracles, and journey with drugs to other, more colourful realms. Old heresies are renewed and others invented, while among all the babble and vanity can be heard certain rediscovered truths, never taught to my contemporaries but absolutely vital to human existence. The greatest of these is an ancient doctrine, now firmly established in all grades of New Age thought, that the universe is an organic system and the earth a divine, living creature. That perception is at the root of true orthodoxy, and from it develops the traditional worldview, which provides the only useful guide to the proper conduct of human affairs.

The world has so obviously changed in forty years that I am amazed by those old college friends who have not revolutionised their thinking accordingly. They should look at what is happening, plain as a pikestaff, under their very noses; at the portents of psychic changes, their effects on minds around them, and the direction in which thoughts are being led. You do not have to be a New Ager to conclude that the only world order in which human nature can happily exist is the sacred order, the cosmological expression of ideal harmony and proportion which constituted the esoteric base behind every ancient lasting civilisation. You cannot yet study it in any state college, but once you have received its principles, which are available spontaneously, you can glimpse the only possible future.

92

The Horror
That Spoils Breakfast

February 1993

The last good breakfast I had was about three years ago. It was a Monday morning, and I went into a café with *The Independent* newspaper to read over egg, bacon, sausage, tomatoes, beans, and chips. In the paper was an article by someone I know, the journalist Andrew Tyler. It was the most horrifying thing I have ever read. Andrew had spent a day at a pig-slaughtering works, modern, EC-approved, all above-board. He went in the early morning to see the pigs kicked and prodded from their farms onto lorries. During the long, jolting drive to the abattoir they sense the horror that awaits them, and the squealing and excreting begins. Inside the noisy, blood-encrusted shed they are seized in front of their fellows and given a stunning charge with electric tongs. This is often ineffective but, conscious and screaming or not, the animals are chained by a hind leg to a machine which carries them into the next room for the throat-cutting ceremony, after which they are dunked into a hot, steaming tank and held under water by men with hooked poles. As Andrew saw for himself, many of the half-stunned, bleeding, terrified animals are actually drowned or scalded to death.

There was much else in the article, including interviews with the wretched, brutalised youths who have to service this holocaust. Their name for the pig is the "horizontal man" because its organs are almost the same as ours. In its habits and character are many human traits; it is almost hairless, and it provides good company. If one was an evolutionist one could plausibly claim the pig, rather than the ape, as our nearest relative.

That for me was the end of bacon and sausage. I swore I would eat no more pig until I had published Andrew's article in my series of radical-traditionalist pamphlets and distributed it as widely as possible about the kingdom. Richard Adams designed the publication, an artist provided some grisly illustrations, and I added an introduction. It was a strong essay against systematic cruelty to animals, pointing out how the terror and suffering inflicted on them poisons the psychic atmosphere of the country and makes it impossible for any of us to be truly happy and at ease. You cannot, of course, avoid some degree of cruelty in dealing with animals. Civilisation is based upon their exploitation, and the only way to prevent it would be to abandon our present way of life and revert to the state of wandering herb-eaters—which is hardly a practical proposition.

Andrew Tyler did not go along with that. True to his convictions he is an honest vegan, avoiding the use or consumption of animals in any way at all. We could not agree on the form of the introduction, and the project was shelved. Thus I was stuck with my vow, unable to issue the publication, which would release me from it and allow me to enjoy a good breakfast.

The only relief I can find is abroad. In Germany recently they set upon the table a dish of cabbage and mashed potato topped with an array of chops and legs of pork, sausages, black puddings, and similar gross delicacies. I ate my share with relish, reasoning that it is no business of mine what the Germans do to their pigs—I'm sure they are very kind—and that it is properly pious while in their company to feast upon their sacred national animal. In England there are no such excuses. I have painfully re-read the Tyler article, including the expurgated bits, which were too hair-raising for *The Independent* to print, and I would rather live on egg and chips for all eternity than subscribe to the hell which he witnessed in the charnel house for pigs.

93

Horrors and Real Horror

January 1998

*T*he first thing that really frightened me was ghosts. Lord Halifax, the ghost story collector, was in favour of them because, he believed, they developed children's imaginations. It was said that he made his gardeners dress up as ghosts and jump out at his children from dark corners. I should never have survived his regime.

Almost as soon as I could read I took to ghost stories and was scared almost to death by them. Like any addict I knew they were bad for me but kept on with them, and when lonely night came I lay at the edge of my cot, ready for instant flight, tense and sweating, staring at the swaying curtain through which at any moment something terrible might appear. My granny said that ghosts were just poor lost souls, and if you met one you should calmly ask what it wanted. That advice seemed no more practical in dealing with the monsters I imagined than with a mad axe-man. These things can kill or drive you mad. A girl I knew was staying in a big old Scottish house. She was wakened by the sound of something dragging along the corridor. It stopped outside her room, the door slowly opened, and the dragging continued. It seemed as if nothing had entered until she looked down on the floor, and there, crawling toward the bed, was something so terrible that she had a fit and spent the next few months in a mental hospital. I do not actually believe in ghosts but am well aware of what they can do to you.

Life since then has offered a succession of terrors, but they have all been man-made and never so real and menacing as the spooks. The first I remember was got up by George Orwell, a damaged Old Etonian, who imagined a people's dictator so powerful and officially benevolent that there was no room to criticise him. Some of his supposed policies, such as metrication, have in fact been implemented, but no Big Brother has been sighted in this country and, if you think of it, he never could prevail because the Queen, who has the allegiance of the Army, would order his dismissal—in the same way as she sacked that disorderly prime minister in Australia. As some wise constitutionalist put it (I think it was Ingleby-Mackenzie of the MCC), she is the Dickie bird of politics.

The next terror was the bomb. Popular belief was that atomic warfare was imminent, that everyone would be killed, and the earth reduced to a radioactive cinder. It was not the Queen who stopped that—perhaps it was Bertrand Russell—but somehow it never happened and we moved on to the next scare: ecology. This blew up in the late 1960s, and from then on we reckoned that the earth was doomed. Her lands were polluted; her seas were poisoned; fish, fowl, and fauna were dying out and our species would inevitably follow. Then there was acid rain, the coming Ice Age (or, alternatively, Global Warming), the AIDS scare (effectively dealt with as the Virus that Never Was in Newill Hodgkinson's brilliant, unpopular book), and the usual wars, famine, pestilence, and disturbances in the heavens that traditionally signal the approaching Last Days. I admire Greenpeace and the heroes who fight against evil, and I would give anything to save the whale, ban the bomb, support the hunt, abolish factory farms, and enjoy the natural paradise that God gave us. But you can no longer scare me. My own death, and return to the world of ghosts, now seems more real and imminent than anything that the worldly doom-prophets can think up. The Stock Exchange could collapse overnight and all over the world; wolf-packs of gangsters could occupy my street; but I am no longer bothered by these fantastic inevitabilities. Only one thing worries me: the collapse of culture, about which I shall write, gruesomely, another time.

What has happened
to time? Why is there now so little of it
compared to the amount there used to be?

94

After Blair, the Antichrist

November 1999

The pious Jamaicans who come to see me on behalf of the Jehovah's Witnesses point out that these present times bear all the signs that in the Bible are associated with the Last Days. Tornadoes and earthquakes, plagues and famines, wars and rumours of wars, kingdom against kingdom; all the dramas that the Scriptures promise are now on stage. And the JWs seem rather pleased with these signs. There will be an almighty disaster, of course, but the righteous will be saved, all 144,000 of us, and we will live to see the restoration of God's kingdom upon earth. But before that time must come the brief reign of Antichrist, the great leader who tries to maintain by force the corrupt old order.

The most immediately interesting character in this scenario is the Antichrist, the first to appear on stage. In II Thessalonians, chapter 2, there is a description of him. "Let no man deceive you," wrote St. Paul. Before the coming of divine rule there will be a "falling away" and the appearance of "that man of sin" who "opposeth and exalteth himself above all that is called God, or that is worshipped; so that he as God sitteth in the temple of God, showing himself that he is God."

Everyone, of course wants to know who this person will turn out to be. A Protestant joke, first cracked by Sir Francis Bacon, is that if the description in Thessalonians were issued to the police, they would arrest the Pope. There could be something in that, because in Revelation, chapter 13, St. John tells of two "beasts" and clearly identifies the second of them as the Church of Rome. The first beast is set up by the second as an idol in the form of a wounded man with a mark on his forehead, and anyone who refuses to worship it is prosecuted. That man, we are told, has a number, "and his number is 666." If you follow John's instructions and count the number of that phrase (by adding the numerical values of the nineteen Greek letters comprising it) you may learn something that theologians keep to themselves. In the symbolism of number, 666 stands for the positive, decisive aspect of mind, for the power of a ruler on earth and the sun in the heavens. Its opposite number is 1080, a lunar number applying to that subtle element in nature which stimulates the imagination and in Christianity is called the Holy Spirit.

Numbers are neither good nor evil in themselves, only in their relationships, which are either harmonious or disproportionate. That is why it is so ridiculous when fanatical, superstitious people take 666 as the number of the Antichrist and look for someone with that number in his name. The Pope has always been the favourite candidate, but Vatican mystics have found the number in Mohammad, Martin Luther, and the Turks, while modern reckonings include IBM computers. Really! I have no time for such nonsense.

But as human societies fragment while technological power intensifies worldwide, the time of the Antichrist may well be now, and his place may well be here, in Britain. As William Blake observed, we always lead the world in these things—and our situation seems ripe for it. The constitution is in a state of flux, the House of Lords is being gerrymandered, the Queen is inert, gays and lesbians set the tone in the Church and the Army, the arts are corrupt, and the sciences in confusion. This is the time for that "strong man" whom the Bible calls Antichrist.

After the Prime Minister's strange speech to the Labour Party conference in September, some commentators suggested that he was preparing himself for the Antichrist role. He never mentioned God but offered himself as a national substitute, proclaiming himself honest and well-intentioned. That is always a bad sign, but I think there is a bigger fish behind him, and that is whom we should look out for.

95

Six-Six-Six and the Coming of the Beast

December 2001

The USA is supposed to be a country of free speech. But according to an article I have just read no one dares exercise it. After the World Trade Center towers went down, Mr. Bush hid in Nebraska and then called the suicide terrorists "cowardly." A television commentator who criticised his choice of epithets was howled down and sacked. And the same happened to other journalists who failed to echo their President's defiant rhetoric. Suddenly America became like the old Soviet Union, where free speech was allowed as long as the state approved of it.

To us old liberals this abnegation of free speech is like a red rag to a bull. It obliges us to repeat what those commentators might have said if they had not been shut up: that the terrorists' coup in America was a masterpiece of imagination, almost perfectly executed. With the minimum of expense and technology an undeclared enemy laid low the chief symbols of a nation's might, its military acropolis in Washington and the grandiose towers of New York, boastfully named the World Trade Center. Thousands of innocent people died horribly, which makes it a human tragedy. But I am not distressed by the fall of the towers. They were asking for it, and they got it, just as Goliath got it from David's low-tech pebble-slinger.

Also asking for it is the unhappy genius who masterminded the outrage. This person—presumed to be Osama bin Laden—has dedicated himself to ending the reign of Satan. By this he means destroying the dominant institutions of Western materialism. Millions of supporters cheer him on and see him as the prophesied leader whose destiny is to purge the world of evil. Millions of others execrate him as a creature of the Devil. A man who can split the world so effectively and bring humanity to the verge of a religious war is either a great prophet or he is the Antichrist.

He could indeed be both at once. In my studies of Revelation I have noticed that the various figures and symbols in the apocalyptic drama, though they seem like total opposites, are actually one and the same or different sides of the same coin. The Whore of Babylon corresponds to the Bride of Jerusalem, the Beast to the Lamb, the Man of Sin in Thessalonians to the Son of Man. The two contrasting cities, Babylon and the holy city Jerusalem, even have the same number when you add up the numerical values of the Greek letters in their names. This implies that they are essentially the same city, with the same good people in them, but in different stages of the cycle that ends in decadence and downfall.

The character in Apocalypse who represents both Antichrist and God's true prophet is known esoterically by the number 666, which is the number of the Beast in Revelation 13. This number is vulgarly associated with pure evil, but symbolic numbers apply to eternal principles and have no moral attributes. In the ancient, scientific code of number, 666 stands for the solar, positive, rational, imperial side of nature—as opposed to 1080, which symbolises the lunar, imaginative aspect of things.

It is plausible to identify bin Laden with 666, in which case he is playing a part that someone has to take on in these apocalyptic times. According to St. John's encoded statement, Jesus played that part at the beginning of the previous age. It is an illusion that these people are either good or evil. The character of 666 is written into the script, and if you are chosen to enact it, bad luck. It means having to rule the world in the pure, unalloyed spirit of 666, which is the fierce energy of a dictator. Then, following the script, you are torn down and sent to hell, and then comes a thousand-year period of divine rule on earth. It is a great drama, as long as you are not acting in it.

What has happened
to time? Why is there now so little of it
compared to the amount there used to be?
into those

96

Prophets,
Saviours, and Fanatics

February 2002

A lady wrote in to *The Oldie* last month complaining about the
previous *Orthodox Voice* where I had drawn parallels between
Osama bin Laden and Jesus Christ. She did not like the comparison
and implied that I was disloyal, bringing comfort to our enemies.

A lot of good people think like that, but I have a problem with
Jesus. Hi-jacked by sentimentalists, remodeled as a kind of New Age
peacenik, the popular Jesus of today is quite unlike the figure of New
Testament record. The man quoted in St. Matthew's Gospel, chapter
10, told his disciples plainly that he was no man of peace. His purpose,
he said, was to stir up trouble, to set son against father, daughter against
mother, and family against family. "Think not that I am come to send
peace on earth," he insisted. "I came not to send peace but a sword."
That could well be bin Laden's mission statement.

As a fundamentalist cult leader, Jesus's mission was to reform his
own people and lead them into the ways of righteousness. He instructed
his disciples to preach only to their fellow Jews, ignoring Gentiles and
Samaritans. They were to promise their converts access to heaven and to
threaten the others with hell. And they had to be ready for persecution
and martyrdom. That is properly called fanaticism. Jesus was executed

for it after his violent attack on the financial community in the Temple precinct, Jerusalem's Trade Center.

If bin Laden's story is to follow that of Jesus, he will be crucified by the authorities, spark off a new religion, and become the son of God to millions of dedicated followers. It will be the same old story once again. I have been reading about that story in a book called *The World's Sixteen Crucified Saviors* by Kersey Graves, first published in 1875 and recently revived by the aptly named publishers, Adventures Unlimited. The story is about a saviour, son of a virgin whose husband was a carpenter; born under a bright star at midwinter, visited by wise men from afar. He was crucified between two thieves, rose from the dead, and redeemed the world from sin. This man was an Indian called Krishna who lived ages before Jesus. It is not just his story but an ancient, universal myth, attached to all founders of great religions. According to Mr. Graves, nothing that Jesus said or did was original or peculiar to him. Everything had been done before, by Krishna, Odin, Mithra, Zoroaster, and many others, and no doubt the same legend will be attached to future saviours, or trouble-makers.

Kersey Graves was a typical rationalist of his time. Having exposed the Jesus story as merely a recurrent myth, he concluded that we can and should get rid of it. He called upon humanity to forget about god-men and saviours and live sensibly by the doctrines of science. The same atheist view is put forth by Richard Dawkins today. But the trouble with atheism is that it does not work. We are not really in control of things. We cannot abolish prophecy, nor can we change the script that makes terrorists into holy martyrs and sons of God. We did not write that script in the first place.

So we have to go along with it. To us innocents, happily enjoying the wealth and luxury of this latter-day Babylon, prophets and religious fanatics are unwelcome. It is quite natural for us to oppose them, to call them irrational and fanatical, to hate them and bomb them and exterminate them. That too is in the script. But something that is not in the script is your own personal perception. You can look at the script for yourself, and you can then see that prophets and terrorists are written into it. They are sent by God the scriptwriter to keep the plot moving, to put down the mighty, scourge the usurers, achieve martyrdom, and save humanity. That sounds like the kind of person we need today.

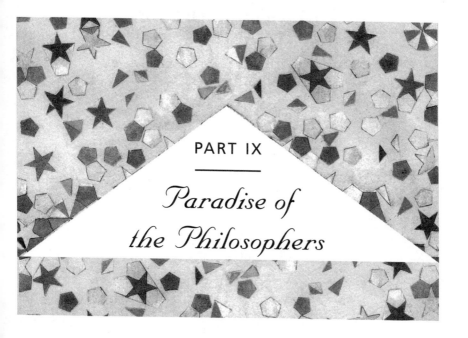

PART IX

Paradise of
the Philosophers

97

Turn On and Tune In
to God's Kingdom

May 1999

*T*here seems to be a row blowing up between our God correspondent, Alice Thomas Ellis, and Sir Ludovic Kennedy, who
says that he is an atheist. She laughs at him for practising the rites of
Scottish dancing, and he laughs at her beliefs in a virgin mother with
a son who walked on water and rose from the dead. It is the same
old argument, and I am surprised that these two senior sages bother
with it.

Kennedy, I feel sure, is a good man, keeps most of the Command-
ments, does not steal, murder, or covet his neighbour's ox and would be
as helpful as any Samaritan if he saw you in trouble by the wayside. He
claims that he does not praise God with all his heart and so on, but I
think that is his delusion. An old person who dances reels and enjoys
a drink in good company can hardly avoid praising the source of his
existence. And if he is such a firm atheist why does he live at Avebury,
the ancient religious centre of southern England?

It is ridiculous for these oldies to quarrel because, whether or not
they profess to believe in God, they are both part of God's Creation
(or his Big Bang, if you like) and enjoy the same divine gift of existence. And they are both heirs to the promise of God's kingdom

restored to earth. Another name for this is the heavenly Jerusalem. Recent experiences in the Holy Land compel me to realise that the reappearance of the ideal city or divinely ordered realm is not just possible but inevitable and actually now in progress. Jerusalem itself is the obvious place where this revelation will occur, but our national prophecy, uttered by William Blake, is that the pattern of sacred order will first become apparent here in Britain—at Avebury, perhaps. That, when it happens, will put an end to quarrels about God and whether or not there is such a thing, because we will experience the true answer with no further need to speculate.

As a mystical idealist I affirm that God and his paradise are within reach of anyone, sometimes coming as a gift, sometimes through a course of study and initiation. States in the progression toward truth and happiness are categorised by Plato. They begin with ignorance, when you do not even realise that there is anything worth knowing. The next state is opinion, and above that is knowledge, meaning study of the various grades of truth, from the conventions of correct spelling to the absolutes of number and geometry. Properly directed, these studies lead toward the fourth stage, that of understanding (Plato's *nous*).

But education cannot take you the whole way. Something further is needed, something that will transform an alert-minded, well-read person into a complete, truth-centred initiate. In the ancient world that purpose was served by the Mysteries, at the core of which was an idealised replication of the near-death experience. Not being a cultist I have no idea whether or where that form of initiation is available today, but there is handy substitute, well adapted to the needs of older, rational, educated people who would like to become wiser, happier, perceptive, tolerant, and free from worries about God and the afterlife. To those good people, mature, ready, and qualified for it, I recommend a dose of your grandchildren's illegal drugs: not that filthy crack and such, but something like Dr. Hofmann's acid or the stuff that Aldous Huxley writes about in *The Doors of Perception*. It cannot harm you now, and it may well prolong both your life and your interest in it. I do not recommend it to callow youths or to those stuck on the levels of ignorance or opinion, but it is just the thing for L. Kennedy, together with Alice T. Ellis. They could do it at Avebury, while the Druids are ritualizing and the Morrismen are dancing outside the Red Lion Inn.

98

What Is the Point of Love?

June 1999

Since this is meant to be a philosophical column—a series of approximations toward truth—there is no avoiding the subject from which Philosophy (love of wisdom) derives one half of her name—the subject of love. Everyone knows how delightful it is and how it makes the world spin round, but there is another, painful side to it, which probably causes more suffering in more people's lives than any other normal experience. Experts declare that the complaint called heartbreak or, by the vulgar, sexual frustration, is the third most excruciating form of pain after gout and childbirth. It is not like the others, a physical pain (though it might as well be), and in our rational minds we know that it is a delusion. But love obsession is unresponsive to reason; it is a kind of mania, and there is no quick, easy cure for it. Germaine Greer put it well and bluntly, "If you think you are 'in love' you are in real trouble." All that specialists can recommend is distance from the beloved, or different company and scenery—the Foreign Legion method of forgetting past love. Time is the natural cure, but it works too slowly to relieve the pain of the frustrated lover.

In two of his works on love, the *Phaedrus* and the *Symposium,* Plato displays its various levels, beginning with the basic desire of one body for another, and culminating in the mystical meeting with love itself, which is the philosopher's orgasm. In between are the stages by which love is extended from one single object to embrace the whole. Then, having completed its expansion, it concentrates again upon one object: the Creator. That implies that all forms of love are aspirations toward love of God, and that the pain you feel on parting with a beloved is the pain of separation from God. You hear that most clearly in popular sentimental songs. They whinge on about lost girls and boyfriends and how lonesome they feel, but the music tells of a deeper yearning, not just for an individual body but for a lost state of perfect love and happiness, only visible in retrospect. That, surely, is the yearning of the soul for a dimly remembered paradise, which could only have been experienced in some previous or prenatal existence. One of the proofs that the soul is immortal, and that we should identify with that component of ourselves rather than with our decaying bodies and declining appetites, is that we experience nostalgia for a lost idyll. As a child, in the drawn-out beauty of long summer evenings, I had moments of sharp, sweet melancholy for a glorious past which I had never actually known. Later, passing through the loneliness and heartbreaks of youth, I found that the pain they brought was much the same as the old nostalgia pain. It is a pain of the soul, and the apparent cause of it is that the soul has fallen from a paradise it once knew.

It seems to me that our souls, with their yearnings and nostalgias, are trying to tell us something, that they are dissatisfied with their lapse from paradise and find it unnatural. They are demanding to be returned to it, not in some future life but here and now. That is a legitimate demand and by no means impossible to satisfy. From personal glimpses and from the best authorities among seers, poets, and philosophers, I have no doubt that earthly life can be viewed and lived as a type of paradise, just as easily as it can be experienced as hell. The difference, I suppose, is to do with love. Being in love gives you a glimpse of paradise, but it cannot be the real thing because it is not lasting, and there is as much pain as there is pleasure in it. For real satisfaction, especially after you have received your seniors' bus pass, there is nothing to beat love of wisdom and, if you are lucky, the philosopher's orgasm.

99
What Good Manners!

April 2001

*R*eaders have been writing to a newspaper about good manners and whether or not they are to be found in modern cities. What strikes me is how different are the experiences they tell about. One old person went out, was pushed and jostled by louts, spilt her shopping, was forced off the pavement, and nearly run over, while another was greeted kindly in shops, had doors held open for her, and was offered a seat in the bus. That is precisely my own experience. One day, as I go about my humble business, I think how kind and graceful my fellow townsfolk are. Next day they slam the door in my face and jump the post office queue.

What do you make of that? As an old-time observer of how the world works, I suspect that the way I am treated is largely my own doing. My Indian friend, who has been stricken with wisdom in his old age, has discovered that if you determine to see this world as a paradise that is how you tend to experience it. The white man, he says, is obsessed with creating utopias—artificial paradises—but our actual paradise is the world just as it is, here and now, if only we would see it.

I have told several friends about his philosophy, and those who have given it a try say that it really does work. There are days when you feel alert, happy, and at peace with all, and those are the days when everyone is polite and the bus comes just as you get to the stop. Other days it seems quite the reverse. But if you have adopted the "paradisal worldview" and are committed to seeing the best in everyone, it is amazing how people conform to the benevolent image that you have imagined upon them.

To me it has become an embarrassment. Seeing my white hair, young waitresses bring my coffee with an infuriating simper, and other young girls, black, white, and Indian, invite me to take their seats on the buses. I suspect they are partly doing it to impress their friends, but these graceful gestures and those I encounter elsewhere, from all kinds of people, prove to me that everyone is trying to do the right thing according to the notion of good manners they have been brought up with.

An example I have just seen was in a provincial pub I went to with an old friend, the headmistress of the local school. As she entered, the slouching youths, many of whom had enjoyed the benefit of her kind-but-strict regimen, sat up straight in the way you are supposed to.

What is the source of good manners? Were you born to act gracious or was it drummed into you? The traditional answer is that, like all aspects of culture, the laws of politeness were divinely given. At one time we were ruled directly by the gods. They were highly refined beings, and very musical. They knew the harmonies that resonate with the best in human nature, and in that age public manners were so exquisitely correct that no actual laws were needed. When the gods left they taught certain people the secrets of how to behave and conduct state affairs. While these standards were upheld, all was well, but we are not good at upholding standards, and gradually everything went downhill.

Yet even in times of chaos the ideals of goodness and righteousness are still apparent in human nature, and if you take up the paradisal worldview you see them predominating. It is only because of this that civil life is possible and still goes on.

Another traditional belief—and I own up to it myself—is that human desire for justice and true standards provokes a response from heaven. So divine rule will one day be restored on earth and perfect manners will once more prevail among us. That, says my Indian friend, is much the way things are here and now. But it takes practice to see it.

100

Life, the Universe, and Everything

April 1998

They say that Mr. Cook, the graceless Foreign Secretary, is a highly intelligent man. I am sorry to hear that because, in my experience, people with a reputation for intelligence are often so misled or incapacitated by the false and elaborate doctrines they have been able to master that they might as well be stupid. Look at Bertrand Russell, for example. His clever reasoning led him to conclude that despair is the only justifiable attitude to life. H. G. Wells was clever enough to reach the same dead end and moaned about it in his last book, *Mind at the End of Its Tether*. Wells was a victim of Darwinism, that virus of the intellect that afflicts so many good minds and displays its symptoms in the modern mind generally. I have broached this subject before, and readers do not always like it, but I write this column for the sake of truth rather than popularity, because that is one way to be happy.

I am constantly surprised by the number of clever, well-educated people who fall under the spell of man-made theories and embrace them with fundamentalist intensity, with no regard for the effect of these chosen beliefs on their own lives and those of their followers. Does Richard Dawkins really believe—against all evidence—that the scientifically dubious faith of Darwinism, with its atheistic connotations, is likely to improve anyone's life? How can Prof. Hawking suppose that his black-hole-studded cosmology—a product only of his own mind—is of any human benefit? Why does the brilliant Jacques Monod think it worth devoting a lifetime to arguing against our spiritual connection with the universe? These theorists are not entirely wrong, but they are arbitrary. Why are they so blind to the consequences of their opinions?

There is a secret behind this, but it is only a secret because modern science cannot live with it, and the modern mind cannot bear to hear it. *Oldie* readers have probably discovered it already, and they will confirm it to neophytes: that the universe has no particular form or character independent of human imagination. As Charles Fort put it, nothing will ever be explained because actually there is nothing to explain. There are an infinite number of ways in which you can see the world and an infinite range of data to support or discredit any of them. You can believe in black holes if you like, or you can believe in angels. I am not a believer, but if I had to choose I would take the latter, because unlike the holes, angels have often been sighted and their influence has generally been for the good.

The universe is like a reflector, so your experience of life depends largely on how you choose to see it. You can prove that for yourself by a dose of paranoia, when your fears and suspicions seem to be confirmed by everything that happens. The same can be observed, more usefully, through practical idealism. Use your cleverness to the advantage of yourself and others. Turn off the television; ignore the worldview of spite and confusion broadcast by the media; forget the grisly theorists; summon up the data which indicate that here and now is our natural paradise; establish that model in your mind by reason and then go out and test-drive it in the street. You may not achieve the vision of the Holy Grail in one day, but at least you will begin to see that there is such a thing, that happiness is the normal human condition, and that heaven on earth is not merely a religious delusion but signifies the natural order of the mind and of the world around it.

I hope Mr. Cook knows his job, which is to visualise harmony among the nations, but I fear he may be too intelligent for that.

101
How to Be Lucky

April 1997

*E*very week I have business which involves taking London's 21 bus, that useful conveyance which runs from Chelsea to Camden Town and through several places in my personal geography. Gradually I have come to notice something very odd and irrational. Every single time I stand at a certain stop, waiting for this bus, another of its kind, sometimes three or four, go by in the opposite direction before mine arrives. It only happens at this one stop, and I am quite sure of the phenomenon because I note it down each time on the back of my cheque book. I cannot explain this nor categorise it except as a localised product of what metaphysicians call Sod's Law, classically illustrated by the falling piece of toast that always hits the carpet marmalade-side down. These trivial nuisances, however much repeated, are not unbearable, and I accept them as token payments for the extraordinary amount of good luck that all of us have enjoyed so far in life. It is no mean feat to have escaped the fatal perils of youth and infancy.

Looking back it is clearly evident that a series of incredible coincidences has shaped my entire life. Did they occur somehow by God's will or did I make them happen? On that question I am totally confused, and very happy to be so, for to dwell contentedly on the fact of our essential ignorance is surely the primordial, most natural and best possible mode of existence.

To get through life you have to be lucky. Everyone knows that, but there are two ways of understanding it, one higher than the other. The lower approach is to attract or ensnare luck using the established techniques of religion, astrology, psychology, or self-promotion. New Age bookshops are awash with writings on these subjects, and sometimes they have a section labeled Prosperity, with books on how to attract luck in the form of money. I have a small collection of these, some of them very persuasive, but in the end they all say the same thing, that to gain money you have to make yourself attractive to it, set your mind upon it, and desire it with the intensity of a lover. That often works, no doubt, but the drawback is that money is not the same thing as good luck, and the mental disposition that attracts the one may repel the other. To bring upon yourself good luck rather than just riches, the appropriate object of your cult is good luck itself. Shorn of its material connotations, good luck is seen to be identical with Plato's "the Good," by which he meant the divine pattern of perfect order and harmony that is dimly reflected in our lower world. Good luck is therefore associated with good order, and that, I believe, gives a useful hint toward being lucky. As we know from the Grail traditions, a cosmologically ordered realm, centred on divine law, receives so much good luck or blessings that in the experience of its inhabitants it is an earthly paradise. There is no such state around where I live, and perhaps you cannot find it anywhere, but it still occurs, individually, in the mind of anyone who cultivates it. From what I have read, heard, and glimpsed, my impression is that you can make good luck flow into your life, and quite easily—provided you no longer want to be lucky and you love God unconditionally, expecting nothing in return. That is what the Quietists used to say, and the Church persecuted them for it, so it is probably true.

In a break from writing the above, I went to that accursed 21 bus stop, and my bus came immediately. So much for superstition! The fare was 80p, and my small change amounted to—would you believe it?—79p. I had to proffer a £10 note, which made the driver scowl and puff. I take this incident as a spontaneous ritual that has changed my luck at the bus stop.

102

Platonic National Service

October 1992

There is no sadder sight, as one travels around the towns and villages of this country, than the gangs of unemployed youths who hang disconsolately around their market crosses. Deprived through education of their imaginations, constantly assaulted by vicious "music" and the crude, loveless images of television, these poor lads see no legitimate outlet for their talents and are placed at the mercy of demons. As they say in the army, "an idle man is a discontented man."

In the 1950s the education process was followed by compulsory national service. There were certain advantages in this. The military regime was less petty and restrictive than life at boarding school, and we enjoyed two years of respite from life's serious purpose of swindling and cheating one's fellows in business. Yet all in all it did seem rather a waste of time.

How much better things were done in Plato's ideal realm. National service, as described in the *Laws,* also lasted two years, but the whole thing was better directed and far more useful. The tradition throughout the ancient world was to divide all the people into twelve tribes, each occupying one of the twelve sections of the country that were dedicated to one of the zodiacal deities. The young men of each tribe were called up in groups of sixty under the command of five officers. Beginning in their home territory, they moved during the course of a year through the entire country, being stationed for a month in each of its sections. At the end of the year they repeated their progress in reverse order, finally ending up at home. In that way, says Plato, they got to know every part of their own country in different seasons.

Some of the duties were military, making and manning the fortifications, but for the most part the young men were engaged in public works. They maintained the roads and hedges and were responsible for drainage and irrigation. Their efforts were not only practical—to supply fresh water to every part of the district—but they were also designed to beautify and sanctify the landscape. They set trees and ornamental buildings along the riverbanks, and wherever water bubbled from the ground from a sacred spring they enclosed it within a meditative grove. An important function was to ensure that a stream of pure water ran through every local temple.

The young men established sports centres with fountains and heated swimming pools. In the summer months they gathered and laid up all the dry wood that was needed for the winter. This, said Plato, was far more useful to the old people and far more beneficial to public health than the administrations of any number of doctors. He did not go on to say, though it may easily be inferred, how pleasant it was for the young men and the local girls to enjoy each other's company for a month or two.

I never thought I would become an advocate for any sort of national service, but it is easy to advocate something which you will not have to do yourself, and Plato's version appears to offer more advantages and less drawbacks than anything else one can imagine. At least it would help the English people to get to know each other, rather than continue as we are, floundering shyly in a morass of race, class, sex, and money inhibitions, which seem far more acute today than they ever were before. A Platonic national service would do more for the culture and harmony of our nation than all our lecturers, social workers, psychiatrists, and policemen put together.

103
Visions of Heaven and Hell

November 1995

This has been a wonderful summer and I have had two visions in it, neither of them supernatural but both seemingly portentous. The first was on the Calf of Man, an islet off the south end of the main island, which Shakespeare seems to have had in mind when he wrote *The Tempest*. A boatman took me there from that poignantly decayed old resort, Port Erin, beloved by John Betjeman, and I spent some happy hours among the former haunts of Caliban the Mooncalf (anag Calf o' Mon), Ariel, and wise old Prospero.

From a high place I saw the boat returning for me and began to run down the slope toward the jetty. Then, far out to sea on the western horizon I glimpsed something that I had often read about in Manx folklore—the legendary Isles of the Blessed, the land of perpetual summer where deserving souls enjoy themselves after death. Clear and flowing in a rose-coloured light, they were just as beautiful as the Celtic seers described them. I could hardly believe my good luck, and as I stood gazing at them I was able to make out details of groves and habitations.

This was too much for the modern mind, and reason soon came to the rescue. What I had taken for the sea horizon was a level band of mist, and the islands above it were the tops of clouds illuminated by a watery sun. My own eye had provided the other features. I was not too disappointed because I had had the experience, and now I know what those Blessed Islands really look like.

The next vision came soon afterward and it was a picture of hell. Travelling by train to Eastern Europe, I missed a connection and had to spend part of the night at the Frankfurt railway station. The whole of its huge forecourt was like a Bosch painting, seething with demons. To the mundane eye they were human, but of terrible aspect—heroin addicts and crack-takers of all nations, scavenging for food and scrounging money with menaces. A policeman ushered me and other respectable travellers, an English Negro and a man from the North Country, into a large glass box where there were seats, and stood guard outside.

Ever since, in the way that UFO contactees are subsequently haunted by Men in Black, I have been infested by these crack-heads. They howl by night in the street below my window and sometimes twitch into the pub I drink in, recognizable by the black clouds that visibly hang over them.

I thought of these poor souls when another journal sent me a book to review, *The Next 500 Years,* by the scientist and science-fiction writer Adrian Berry. This innocent person supposes that we will shortly be colonizing other planets, shooting through "black holes" in time to appear instantaneously in distant galaxies, and spending holidays in vast hotels revolving in space. His cover shows a sinister hi-tech city of the future in which, as in a typical Hitler watercolour, no people are depicted.

Mr. Berry's new world is unsullied by irrational, untidy human material; it is run by "intelligent robots." This bleak, sterile perception of reality seemed similar to that of the crack-takers, and I detect in both cases the same underlying cause, callow materialism. If only these people could have the vision of the Blessed Isles they would see what the ideal world really looks like, and that would greatly improve the quality of their minds and lives.

There are no black holes there, no ugly robots, and if there are any drugs they must be of sublime quality, like the soma enjoyed by the gods. Those islands look nearer and more easily reachable than any miserable galaxy in outer space. As the artist Peter Blake once said to a Marxist critic who reproached him for lack of realism because he painted fairies, "My fairies are just as real as your revolution."

104
Mirrors of Celestial Harmony

November 1993

The Dean of Canterbury and his Canon for Visitor Care wrote to *The Times* (4 October) in response to an article by the religious correspondent, who had referred to cathedrals as "mirrors of celestial harmony." This phrase was quoted scornfully by the two divines. "Whatever that means," they added.

I was surprised to see that a Dean of Canterbury did not know what a cathedral was for—and that he should be so proud of not knowing as to snub the person who reminded him of it. That, I am sorry to say, is an example of the most serious kind of ignorance, the kind that does not even know, or want to know, that there is such a thing as knowledge. The reason I am sorry to say it is that this Dean is probably a most holy theologian, a dutiful custodian, respectable and right-thinking, whereas I just sit here smoking and carping.

It did not take me long to realise that the Dean and his friend were just pretending to ignorance. It is a clerical subterfuge by which they try to make us believe that they are just ordinary, simple people like us. Of course they know that cathedrals are mirrors of celestial harmony, and they have only to read their own scriptures (e.g., Ezekiel 43:10; Revelation 11:1) to understand exactly what that means. Throughout both Old and New Testaments are numerous injunctions to those who desire initiation into the mysteries of priestly religion that they should

289

measure the temple and see for themselves the perfect scheme of proportions by which it was created.

The perfectly proportioned temple is, of course, the universe, a divinely made creature containing all opposite and rationally irreconcilable elements within a perfectly functioning organism. That was the model which was imitated by the builders of state temples throughout the ancient world, and the pagan tradition of sacred architecture was inherited by the guilds of Masonic craftsmen who constructed the mediaeval cathedrals. Their esoteric knowledge, reserved for those they initiated in their lodges, was a science of number, harmony, and proportion; their particular use for it was in building churches and cathedrals in such a way that those who entered them received the impression of an earthly paradise.

To create this impression every form of the art contributed its finest products. In the calm light of eternity, diffused through stained glass windows, every part of the building was carved and painted to represent the entire spectrum of existence, from spiritual certainties to the rough-and-tumble of everyday life. The Dean need only peep at the misericords beneath the seats of his cathedral choir to see types of that celestial harmony of which he pretends to know nothing. The choir was at the very heart of the cathedral, for the whole edifice was a generator and broadcaster of divine influence, and the trained voices of human choristers are the nearest we can ever get to the ideal, angelic chorus.

At the root of all the techniques of priestcraft synthesised in a cathedral was the Masonic science of proportion. By the geometrical canon of that science, combined with the numerically calculated powers of harmonics, the masons threw great stones into the air and held them, vaulted aloft, in a fabric designed to amplify the religious spirit raised within it. That spirit is no longer raised (Protestant rites being the merest shadow of an invocation), so the Dean is probably right in seeing his cathedral as an object of tourism. Yet, if you half-close your eyes, modern tourists seem no different from mediaeval pilgrims; and the reason they visit a cathedral is probably the same as ever, to experience the celestial harmony.

105
Totally Stoned

August 2000

On June 1, 1985, a mob of amphetamine-crazed riot police set upon a party of festival-goers on their way to celebrate the midsummer sunrise at Stonehenge, smashing their vehicles and arresting 600 of them. The victims were white and British, so there was no question of institutionalised racism, but there are other types of discrimination and some of them are so deeply institutionalised among us that they are hardly questioned. One such is the official prejudice that favours big business over popular rights and interests. This means that Stonehenge is administered for the benefit of tour operators and English Heritage trinket-sellers, while those who maintain its tradition as the national temple and place of midsummer assembly have been kept away from it by force.

This year, however, in response to all kinds of pressure, not least from the European Court, there was a change of policy. The Stones were thrown open to all and anarchy was given its day. I had to see this, so made my way through the pubs of Salisbury and took a lift up to the Plain and entered the great circle where a large, rough-looking crowd was vibrating to the rhythm of native drummers. The drumming went on all night, drowning out the efforts of various white-robed Druid groups to perform their ceremonies. Good for anarchy! I thought. These people have rejected priestcraft and are awaiting that divine revelation of cosmic order that provides the only laws that honest people can live by.

Despite the cold drizzle, this and other benevolent thoughts filled my head, and I experienced a night of enchantment. One reason for that, perhaps, was an incident that happened early on. The government had arranged for a dim red light to glow at the end of the Stonehenge Avenue, anticipating the dawn sunrise, and I asked some people standing on a fallen stone to help me up so that I could see it better. Having done so I began to climb down, but a clumsy hippy intruded his assistance and grabbed my hand, causing me to swing in an arc and hit my head on the stone opposite. Blood came out, my cap and spectacles flew away into the night, but the effect of the blow was to clear my mind and open it to a deeper understanding. I felt love for everyone I saw there, the old friends, the brave anarchists, the spiritual revivalists and Druids, the police, freemasons, and their plainclothes colleagues in football-hooligan outfits. And I could not but love the rough young girls with their bare, skinny, tattooed limbs. It was that "peak experience" extolled by Mr. Maslow and Colin Wilson. It was something like the meeting with "love itself" that Socrates in the *Symposium* promises to initiates.

It may have been the drumming, the blow on the head, the Stonehenge vibes, or midsummer mania, but however it came I received a message, which I pass on to all who expect some creative issue from this experience. Here it is. "We white nations have destroyed our own cultures to the extent that we can hardly talk, sing, dance, think, or look after ourselves properly. Yet we are hell-bent on spreading our mental sickness through Asia and Africa, ravishing their economies, driving their country people into urban slums, and using their lands for mass-scale, chemically engineered food production. Why is this? The answer is that it is a racket. It is a profitable racket, popular with the rich and powerful, who call it "Saving the World." But the world does not need to be saved. Nature can look after her own interests, and those who live by nature and their own native cultures can do the same. The thing that needs saving is the white man's soul. So he should pipe down, keep his bossiness to himself, and cultivate his own salvation in the lands that the gods have allotted for his portion of paradise."

This may be a channeled message, but it is also what I think myself.

106
More Tea, Vicar

February 1995

Some people at *The Oldie* are complaining that there is too little honest writing about drugs. Many writers who have been influenced by them hardly mention that in public, as if the subject were tacitly forbidden. There are, of course, several forbidden subjects and many unprintable points of view, and these I never raise for fear of the wrath of zealots. Questioning the authorship of Shakespeare has been my bravest effort so far. But drugs have been a powerful force in directing modern thinking. Though mostly illegal, there they are, and there we are with them, so it is only practical to accept the phenomenon and consider such questions as why it came and what is it for?

The older you get, try as you may, the more sensible and right-thinking you become, and the more inclined to adopt the orthodox, religious view of things. The religious view is that everything that happens is by God's will and ultimately for our common good, though we do not always see it that way at the time.

Traditional philosophy says much the same, except that it brings no one's will into it but describes in alchemical terms the processes by which necessary changes are effected. Inventions and innovations occur when the spirit of the age demands them. The Age of the Wheel, when

294

it arrived, brought forth wheels, and the Age of Steam steam trains, rather than, or as well as, the other way round.

When the Age of Drugs dawned, the inevitable followed. Its dawning in the middle of the 1960s was apparent from the new modes of music, dress, thought, and conduct that came with it. It is interesting to recall the responses to it at the time—some people marching off to rebuild socialism, some seeking the embrace of Earth on a smallholding in Wales, and many believing in the approaching Millennium, when everything would suddenly be transformed into its ideal, as described in the Book of Revelation.

I personally acquired the millenarian perception, and have ever since borne witness to it through studies in the ancient codes of knowledge, which, together with the transcendent vision, are said to be the basic ingredients of the Holy Grail.

The most powerful catalyst was lysergic acid, discovered and tested by that Promethean hero, Dr. Hofmann of Switzerland. It claimed a number of casualties, but far less than that poisonous lager, that stupid, swindling cocaine, and the unspeakable crack. To those who were ready for it, it brought liberation on the philosophical, cosmological level, a sense of religious awe, and other lasting benefits. These gifts come with responsibilities and, if they are wasted or used for any other purpose than serving the spirit, they bring damnation. My own experience is that any drug can be put to good use, for exploring different ways of seeing things and enlarging one's picture of reality to accommodate them. Any drug used merely for sensual pleasure is more or less deadly. Boredom and vanity are the quickest killers.

It is difficult to find the orthodox line on drugs. Plato, to whom one naturally turns first, has nothing to say except that drinking parties—and perhaps he would also have included acid trips—should be controlled by a sober person to keep the talk and action in tune with harmony. He would probably have approved of the Ecstasy drug, but only for senior citizens, for injecting love and understanding into discussions with old friends. No doubt he had his own classically refined ancient drugs, but like all respectable writers kept the details to himself. Modern analysis of his work suggests that he partook heavily of hashish, from that soothing, God-given herb that has ever afterward been known as the Philosopher's Friend.

107

Buried Treasures

August 2001

*T*here is a certain kind of bookshop, most common in the United States, which specialises in New Age subjects. There are sections on pyramids, fortune-telling, women's empowerment, and so on, but the one I always make for is labeled "Prosperity." The books in it are about how to become rich.

It is an irresistible subject and many of the books contain useful advice on how to do well, but they all emphasise that if you really want to attract wealth you have to concentrate on it, work and pray for it, think and dream about it, to the exclusion of everything else. This violates the second Commandment (against idolatry), and in any case I have no time for such devotions. So wealth and I remain strangers, which is probably how it was meant to be.

But you can easily become rich without having to sacrifice your soul. According to the experts, there are six different ways of acquiring money:

1. By honest work, craft, or trade.
2. By robbing, swindling, or unlawful dealings.
3. By winning it through gambling or lottery.
4. By marrying it.

5. By inheriting it.

6. By finding it.

The first way is the most respectable but it tends to be slow and laborious. The second, getting rich through crime, puts you always in fear of the law and sets you on the path to hell. Gambling is a nasty occupation and lottery winners are well known for being miserable. And if you marry for money you have to live with someone you do not care for who despises you.

There is much to be said for family inheritances. I often hear it from an old friend, a Suffolk farmer, who disapproves of rich people except for those who have inherited their estates. On the other hand, young heirs are easily corrupted, and there is no stupider waste of time than waiting for the death of a rich relation. The Victorians liked to rub that in with their dramas about a missing will.

This sets up the subject I want to come to—the finding of lost riches. I do not mean grave robbery or the sort of archaeology that brings down curses upon those who do it, but coming across a hidden treasure that no one else has claim to. There can hardly be anything more thrilling than to uncover a precious hoard and draw ancient objects out of the earth. That is how I would most like to become rich.

There is a spiritual basis to this yearning for treasure. One of my favourite subjects is the legend of the lost gold mine. It is not just a legend but a repeated occurrence in all mining areas. A common version is that a young prospector in the mountains finds a cavern full of gold-bearing ore. He takes samples and, after marking the spot, goes to town to have it assayed. It proves to be of high value and the finder is due to make a fortune. But when he returns to stake out his claim, difficulties arise. He cannot find the cave or his mark, and he is not even sure which valley it was in. Years later he is still searching, urged on by the vision of gold glimpsed in his youth. It reminds me of *Pilgrim's Progress*.

The treasure I would most like to find is the library of Glastonbury Abbey. In it were books and documents from Saxon and even earlier times. It was venerated by scholars. Just before the Abbey's dissolution in 1539 its library disappeared, and not a single book from it has been seen since. Evidently it was hidden by the Abbot, somewhere nearby, and that is why he was charged with concealing abbey treasure and hanged. To find that lost treasure would be more rewarding than any amount of wealth.

108

Finding Firm Ground

October 1996

The world is not just full of mysteries, it is more or less made up of them. You can spend a happy life playing detective, investigating the murders of Kennedy, Admiral Somerville, or Lizzie Borden's parents, seeking the identity of Shakespeare, Jack the Ripper, or Anna Anderson, studying UFOs, yetis, crop circles, cattle mutilations, strange coincidences, Loch Ness monsters, or any other aspects of human experience. Or you can turn scientific and ask how the world began and about the origins of life, mind, and culture. Each of these subjects has its authorities, its counter-authorities, and a fringe of hopeful theorists. These people are full of information and expertise, but all they really have to offer is opinions. Properly speaking they are mythmakers, and the object of their game is to establish their particular myth, gain wide, official acceptance for it and thus make it, at least for a time, "real." Behind this attempt to make one's beliefs seem real is the misplaced desire to acquire reality for one's self. That is impossible because the self is only a transient phenomenon, no more substantially real than one's opinions. People like Richard Dawkins, the crusading atheist, go round proclaiming theories, trying to attract reality to their beliefs and thus to themselves, but their efforts are no more than pathetic pretensions. In the world of phenomena there is nothing permanent or constant, so there is no true reality in it, and unreality neither requires nor permits any kind of definitive explanation.

The only way I know of escaping from the world of opinions and theories into the realm of everlasting truth is through the study of number and its graphic expression, geometry. Myths of origin throughout the world tell of a Creator who worked by reference to a certain code of number, implying that numbers existed before there was anything physical for them to number. They are useful, of course, for counting things, but essentially they represent qualities. Six, for example, is called perfect (being the sum of its factors) and repetitive (because its powers always end in six), and for these and other reasons its influence is apparent in inorganic forms of nature, such as the snowflake, the honeycomb, and the six-faceted crystal, whereas Five and its derivative, the "golden section" proportion, are characteristic of organic growth. That is why the rose and most other flowers have five petals. Because Five is the emblematic number of humanity, the dodecahedron, the solid figure made up of twelve pentagonal sides, represents the ideal earth, harmoniously divided between the twelve races of mankind.

Number and geometry are always the same in every age and every corner of the universe. They can therefore be called real, and their reality is reflected in the way of thinking that develops naturally from their study. As you discover how to bring together the heavenly circle and the earthly square, and then how to reconcile the various orders of shape and number within one cosmological figure, your mind becomes changed, greatly to your benefit. The quibbles and contradictions of empirical science no longer distress you, and you appreciate more and more the skilful and beautiful art by which the Creator brought the world into being.

Plato claimed that through the practice of number and symbolic geometry you can sanctify both yourself and your surroundings. If you cannot or do not want to engage in such studies, he continued, the best alternative is simple faith in God because, on his (Plato's) word as an initiate, "things are far better taken care of than you can possibly imagine." That is the best myth I know, and with every year that passes I see ever more clearly that it is the nearest possible approximation to the truth.

The Geometer No. 1. *Tempera painting of John Michell by Maxwell Armfield, ca. 1971.*

APPENDIX

Dynamic Symmetry in the Work of Maxwell Armfield

By John Michell

This essay originally appeared in the exhibition catalogue *Maxwell Armfield 1881–1972*, published by the Southampton Art Gallery, 1978.

Maxwell Armfield spent seven years in America from 1915 to 1922. Halfway through that period, while in New York, he attended a course of lectures given by Professor Jay Hambidge on the usefulness to artists of a system of proportion, Dynamic Symmetry, which he claimed to have discovered from analysis of the works of ancient Egyptian and Greek artists, craftsmen, and architects. A strong group of American painters at the time, including George Bellows and Robert Henri, were working under the influence of Hambidge's theory. Armfield joined them. Throughout the rest of his long life he remained Hambidge's loyal and active disciple.

Jay Hambidge, born in Canada in 1867, became an artist after an early career in journalism. In 1900 he acquired a patron who sent him to Europe to test out certain ideas he had formed about a mathematical secret behind ancient Greek design. The existence of an esoteric canon of proportions among the Egyptians is referred to by Plato, but all attempts to discover its content proved inadequate. In the measured dimensions of the Parthenon and numerous Greek and Egyptian arte-facts Hambidge reckoned he had found it. The reason why others had failed was that they had been looking for the sort of ratios given by the regular figures of two-dimensional geometry—"static symmetry" Hambidge called it—whereas the answer lay in the "dynamic" ratios used in plotting curves. Hambidge published his conclusions in *Dynamic Symmetry* (1917), followed three years later by a book on the propor-tions of Greek vases. For a short time from November 1919 he put out a magazine, *The Diagonal,* with the object of spreading knowledge of dynamic symmetry and of encouraging its use by artists and designers. His entire time was given up to studying the subject and writing and learning about it. Poverty and the obduracy of his critics drove him at times to despair, but support was provided by his group of admirers and by his devoted wife, who later continued his work in a community of artists and craftsmen she founded in North Georgia. Hambidge died in 1924 of a stroke while on the lecture platform.

Maxwell Armfield used to say that when he first heard about dynamic symmetry it was like being reminded of something known long ago and temporarily forgotten. As a theosophist he subscribed to Plato's belief that knowledge of harmony and proportion dwells natu-rally within every human mind and is not so much learnt as recollected. The use of dynamic symmetry, he found, gave new strength and cer-tainty to the composition of his paintings, particularly in alliance with the symbolic and mythological themes that attracted him. He based all subsequent work on Hambidge's system and became its most articulate proponent. His essays and lectures on dynamic symmetry, published in various art journals, are summarised in his book *Tempera Painting Today* (1946), and his interpretation of the mystical philosophy behind it is to be found in his treatise on allegorical geometry, *The Wonder Beyond,* published in 1969 under his theosophical name, Mayananda.

The essence of dynamic symmetry, as applied by Armfield to the design of pictures, is quite simple. It consists of a number of related proportions, which Hambidge called "dynamic," because they occur in the processes of natural growth. They are the successive ratios between unity and the square roots of successive numbers, as 1:√2, 1:√3 1:√4 and 1:√5. To the last of these is related the famous "golden section" ratio, 1:1.618x or 2:(√5-1), which Hambidge added to his canon, explaining that the effect of these "irrational" numbers is to relate the different *areas* of a composition together rather than to give commensurability of line. He believed that the use of these proportions was confined to the Egyptians and Greeks; that it had lapsed by the start of the Christian era; and that if modern artists and craftsmen would plan their work in accordance with the old dynamic ratios they would produce masterpieces to rival those of the ancients.

An objection commonly brought against Hambidge's advocacy of dynamic symmetry in design was that "formulas are not of use to the free spirit," or that an artist's expression of his independence and individual genius is compromised if he must attend to laws of proportion. To this view of things both Hambidge and Armfield were vehemently opposed. Both deplored the "cult of personality" in art, whether resulting in trite realism or in formless projections of individual mentalities. Hambidge wrote, "Art is not nature, but it must be based on nature, not upon the superficial skin, but upon structure. Man cannot otherwise be creative, be free. As long as he copies nature's superficialities he is a slave." Armfield who frequently, in writing and conversation, expressed distaste for all the fashionable art movements of his time, and claimed that as far as his own work was concerned Van Gogh might never have existed, was scathing toward Hambidge's critics. He answered them characteristically:

If anyone fancies that the use of such a guide will cramp his style, be in any way restrictive or limiting, his only course is to try it. If correctly and objectively employed, he will very soon find that it is in fact precisely the opposite in its effect, giving him a freedom and stimulation of his design-faculty he had never known before. Ideas, so much more "original" than any he could think up on his own, will flow easily into his mind from the "original" source of all proportion and its resulting beauty. Of course if he believes his duty or pleasure to be in the recording of the chaotic and meaningless surface of a revolting existence, the method is clearly not for him, though even so it would clarify the mess in which he was floundering and so render his works of some slight interest perhaps.

Several aspects of Hambidge's historical understanding of dynamic symmetry were questioned by Armfield and, more fundamentally, by others. It is now apparent that the ancient use of dynamic proportion was not confined to Greece and Egypt, nor was the tradition ever entirely lost. Renaissance architects, drawing on esoteric sources, combined musical and dynamic proportions in their building plans. Palladio in the sixteenth century recommended the root-two rectangle for the proportions of rooms. Yet even if the ancient canon of proportion was more widely known and more elaborate in its content than Hambidge supposed, such criticisms do not affect the essence of his thesis. The value of his work may be judged by its results. The study and practice of geometry, as Plato declared, leads inevitably to the growth of a sense of proportion, to the benefit of both character and art. It was claimed in Hambidge's time that in American art schools, where dynamic symmetry was taught, the overall standard of design was thereby improved. Many of his students, like Armfield, found that their perceptions, philosophy, and artistic sensibilities were widened by the influence of dynamic symmetry and the ideas Hambidge associated with it. There are some people who seem temperamentally attracted to the study of design archetypes in nature as models for human artefacts, and there are others to whom it has no appeal. Yet even such dull folks, thought Armfield, could benefit from a course of dynamic symmetry. The words he used were: "No method can make a silk purse out of a sow's ear, but this one can at least make the sow's ear less repulsive."

About John Michell

(1933–2009)

John Michell, ca. 2003.
Photo by Carlos Freire

John Michell was born in London in 1933 and educated at Eton and Trinity College, Cambridge. A pioneer researcher and specialist in the field of ancient, traditional science, John Michell is the author of more than 40 books that have profoundly influenced modern thinking. Michell's legacy began when his interest in UFOs inspired the 1967 book *The Flying Saucer Vision,* which then led to his breakout work *The View Over Atlantis* in 1969. It was this book, which connects sacred sites, number and proportion, UFOs, and forgotten knowledge of ancient traditions and myths, that placed John Michell at the center of the British counterculture and New Age movement.

Those two books, along with their sequel *The City of Revelation* (1971), provided a context for the alternative views that were germinating at the time and brought new, underground ideas into the mainstream.

In his later work, Michell wrote extensively about the metaphysical and spiritual qualities of the universe—those universal truths that are codified in nature and continually rediscovered, from ancient times to today. He explored the sacred numbers and geometry found in nature and in spiritual mysteries, such as Fibonacci spirals and the golden angle and the divine city of the New Jerusalem. According to Michell, "Wherever you look, in archaeology and ancient history or in the modern records of parapsychology and strange phenomena, you find evidence to contradict every theory and 'certainty' of official science. The real world is quite different from the way our teachers describe it, and it is a great deal more interesting."

In addition to his published books, he was the author of numerous humorous short treatises and articles in publications as diverse as the *International Times, The Temenos Academy Review,* and *The Spectator.* Since 1997, he wrote a column of humor, philosophy, and social commentary in Britain's *The Oldie* magazine, the basis of which form this anthology. In 2003 an exhibit of his geometrical and other watercolour paintings was held in London at the Christopher Gibbs Gallery.

John Michell died April 24, 2009, at the age of 76 just before publication of his final work, *How the World Is Made.*

> *"Look behind the chaos of our existence and you see order. It is not utopian, fascistical or like any kind of man-made order, but divine and perfect, and it existed before time. Socrates called it the 'heavenly pattern' which anyone can discover, and once they have found it they can establish it in themselves."*
>
> JOHN MICHELL

As we watched, the pattern started falling apart, and soon the work of a lifetime had become a total ruin

Someone must have hit the right note, because everything suddenly began falling into place

The Pattern. *Atlantis, the growth of its pentangle constitution, and (upside down) its fall. Watercolour and collage by John Michell.*

BOOKS OF RELATED INTEREST

How the World Is Made
The Story of Creation according to Sacred Geometry
by John Michell
with Allan Brown

The Dimensions of Paradise
Sacred Geometry, Ancient Science, and the Heavenly Order on Earth
by John Michell

Harmonies of Heaven and Earth
Mysticism in Music from Antiquity to the Avant-Garde
by Joscelyn Godwin

Athanasius Kircher's Theatre of the World
His Life, Work, and the Search for Universal Knowledge
by Joscelyn Godwin

The Harmony of the Spheres
The Pythagorean Tradition in Music
by Joscelyn Godwin

Atlantis and the Cycles of Time
Prophecies, Traditions, and Occult Revelations
by Joscelyn Godwin

Return to the Brain of Eden
Restoring the Connection between Neurochemistry and Consciousness
by Tony Wright and Graham Gynn
Foreword by Dennis J. McKenna, Ph.D.

The Esoteric Secrets of Surrealism
Origins, Magic, and Secret Societies
by Patrick Lepetit
Foreword by Bernard Roger

INNER TRADITIONS • BEAR & COMPANY
P.O. Box 388
Rochester, VT 05767
1-800-246-8648
www.InnerTraditions.com

Or contact your local bookseller